W9-AVK-482

İNTERVIEW
INTERVENTION

Communication That Gets You Hired

Andrew LaCivita

A milewalk Business Book

To Mom and Dad,
for nurturing my undying will to succeed
and teaching me that failure doesn't exist.

CONTENTS

Research yourself first and the company second. Results from thousands of recruitment calls and interviews show that people approach the job search backward. Learn how to address your needs to ensure you know the job you want before—not after—the fact. Discover how to conduct research to uncover the most pertinent information related to the potential employer to determine whether the company is right for you.

There are three reasons you actually get the job. Unfortunately, you can only control one of them. Newsflash—your qualifications get you an interview. They have virtually nothing to do with getting you the job. Learn how to influence the three factors that affect job attainment: 1) the candidate's ability to effectively articulate qualifications and potential contributions (encoding), 2) the interviewer's ability to accurately interpret the candidate's qualifications (decoding), and 3) the interviewer's capacity to remember the candidate (memory). Uncover the biases that contribute to these factors and learn how memory works so you can craft stories the interviewer will remember.

Chapter 3
The Two Types of Questions
22

Interviewers want to know either what you did or what you will do. Every question, however disguised, falls into one of these two categories. Learn how to recognize the question type and respond appropriately to overcome the interviewer's most common blind spot.

Chapter 4
"Friending" the Interviewer
27

The fastest way to develop a connection is to shrink the world. The most effective is to share the same passion. Discover techniques to establish a connection with the interviewer from the onset and learn how to identify similar interests to eliminate the detriment of the doubt and realize the benefit of the doubt.

Chapter 5
Storytelling
31

Say it so they get it. Say it so they remember it. Say it so they want it. The encoding and decoding issues are further exacerbated by the interviewer's need to tap long-term memory to recall the candidate. Learn to incorporate the six key qualities that make your stories accurate and memorable: 1) keep it short and simple, 2) capture and keep their attention, 3) talk in their lingo, 4) make them believe you, 5) get them to care, and 6) get them to act.

Chapter 6
My "Silver Bullet" Interview
43

How you say what you say is just as important as what you say. Apply the storytelling principles to any interview question. Learn the fourteen most effective interviewing questions, the rationale behind them, and the most effective responses.

Chapter 7
Profit from Questioning—Sell Twice, Buy Once

In an interview, waste no time doing anything that doesn't help sell you—not even when asking questions. Learn how to organize your questions to reanswer interviewing questions without uttering a single word. Review the most effective way to structure questions to maximize the benefits of selling yourself and gathering intelligence. Ensure you are getting pinpoint answers and making the best use of your time during the segment of the interview you actually control. Learn over forty great questions to ask the employer.

Chapter 8
Closing Time

Start closing when you walk in the door, and don't stop closing until you pull the door shut on your way out. Learn the best techniques to close an interview so you leave no doubt in the interviewer's mind that you are the right candidate for the job. Address any interviewer reservations that might have surfaced due to communication gaps. Review techniques to help reassure the interviewer that it is okay to hire you.

Chapter 9
Decision Time

You have been logical up until this point. Why become emotional now? Ensure you are well-positioned to review an employment offer, maximizing your two greatest assets—self-awareness and intuition— to help you make the right decision. Learn how to handle the sensitive compensation question.

Chapter 10
The Breakup

Prepare for the kitchen sink even if they don't throw it at you. Review the most effective techniques and communication methods for both verbal and written resignations.

Chapter 11
Wait! Don't Leave!

Accepting a counteroffer grants you a shelf-life of six to twelve months. If you accept a true counteroffer, you might as well start interviewing again—immediately. Review what actually transpires during the counteroffer stage, including your and the company's emotional roller coaster, economic impacts, and integrity issues. Recognize the potential aftermath of the renegotiation as it relates to you and them.

Chapter 12
If You Interview Today

Use this short summary guide as a checklist to help navigate you through the interviewing process.

PREFACE

A few days before I submitted the manuscript of this book to Balboa Press, my father and I were sitting at his kitchen table. He asked, "Why did you decide to write the book?" The question was simple enough. Even so, I immediately felt the wave of reasons hit me at a speed that would make your hair stand up. I responded to him in the shortest, most encapsulated way I could: "Because I cannot possibly reach the number of people that could benefit from what I've learned without putting it on paper. Helping a few people each day simply isn't good enough for me."

An idea for any book rarely surfaces in an instant. This one evolved over a few years. It took time and energy. As you can imagine, there was also significant trial and error in building these methods. Along the way, I learned many things, but there was one constant that kept driving me—I genuinely feel people deserve great things in life, especially when it comes to their career. I wanted to help them secure that, which is a large part of why I became an executive recruiter. It's the feeling I put into every preparation call or meeting I conduct with candidates prior to their job interview. This book is my attempt at providing you an inside look so that it might benefit you as well.

The book itself was much easier to write than I thought it would be. Not because it required little effort, but because I've spoken these words to thousands of candidates I've prepared for interviews over the years. Each time, I was unconcerned about them saying something silly or how it would reflect upon on our organization. My fear was more analogous to a criminal defense lawyer with an innocent client (without the consequences, of course). I was far more concerned that a candidate we had spent several hours evaluating, who was qualified and was a great fit for an organization we were representing, would not secure a job because of something the candidate or interviewer misrepresented or misinterpreted.

As I wrote the book, I often thought of this funny story my good friend Laura told me one day while we were having lunch. She said, "Andy, I went to my hairstylist the other day. I said to him, 'John, I can never get my hair as good as you do.' His response was, 'I certainly hope not.'" She has a great relationship with him, so he obviously meant this tongue-in-cheek, that he hopes she continues to see him because of his professional expertise. This is how he earns his living. I tried to keep that same central theme by remembering you, the readers, whether a job candidate or interviewer, do these activities very infrequently throughout your work lives. I do this, or at least monitor it, every day of mine. I wanted to highlight the key concepts you could call upon during your career change or interviews and also develop them in a manner that you could apply to any form of communication—whether it is with your spouse, friend, coworker, or the public.

Speaking of the public, shortly before I completed the manuscript, I discovered this quote by Winston Churchill: "Writing a book is an adventure. To begin with, it is a toy and an amusement; then it becomes a mistress, and then it becomes a master, and then a tyrant. The last phase is that just as you are about to be reconciled to your servitude, you kill the monster, and fling him out to the public." The first thing I thought was, "This? From Mr. 'I have nothing to offer but blood, toil, tears, and sweat?'" Well, after I got over my initial shock, I reflected on my daily journey of preparing this book. Churchill was pretty much dead on with one exception. I did experience most of those things. It was an adventure that provided me with a great deal of fun and enjoyment. Some days this book felt like my only friend, and other days it felt like a coliseum full of people yelling. But instead of trying to kill it, I wanted to give it life and set it free.

I hope you will respond to me in some way, so that I know it helped you. For me, that is the only thing that will ultimately assure me that my journey was worth it.

ACKNOWLEDGMENTS

I am never at a loss for people to thank for my good fortune. Whether you are someone I speak with every day, a business colleague or friend I connect with a few times each year, or a reader who has sent me an occasional e-mail, I cherish you all and greatly appreciate the experiences you have shared with me.

To my parents, Michael and Emilia, thank you so much for all the love and support throughout my life. I truly won the parents' lottery. Dad, remember, Robert Henri said, "Do whatever you do intensely." To my siblings, Danielle, Michele, and Rocco, thanks for keeping our family unit tight and naming a few of your children after me.

To the entire milewalk team, thanks for being the most wonderful group of individuals anyone could ever ask to work with. A special thanks to Kara Dziedzic for being my rock and always keeping me steady. You are the definition of a true teammate and friend. To Carrie Oser, I could not manage without you. Thank you for helping me with all facets of my work and personal life.

To the many milewalk clients we've worked with over the years, I'm grateful to you all for allowing us to support you and providing us with experiences I was able to channel into this book. Although there are too many to name individually, I would like to send a special thank you to some that have treated us as genuine partners (named alphabetically): Liz Anderson, Sam Biardo, Karen Bolton, Linda Bracken, Beth Cabrera, Jackie Fairleigh, Mark Federman, Vito Fiore, John Fix, Jay Fought, Mary Lynn Godee, Kris Hackney, Aaron Howell, Suzette Jaskowiak, Kevan Jedlowski, Troy Johnson,

Alex Kormushoff, Patrick Payne, Jennifer Paraskos, R. J. Reimers, Dave Rosevelt, Tom Snapp, Paul Stillmank, Drew Shields, John Schmidt, Bob Schmitt, Adam Weyeneth, Steve Winchester, and Dave Zaret. I would also like to single out Ted Goodman, who has helped me and milewalk in countless capacities. I am eternally thankful for your support and friendship.

To the very many milewalk candidates we've helped over the years, I do what I do because of you. Thanks so much for your support and educating us as much as we teach you. Thanks too for helping me with the statistics, intelligence, insight, and scads of other information that allows us to more effectively help the next person. A special thanks for all the referrals to additional people that help us as well.

To my dear friend, Laura Wilkens, thank you for helping me throughout this entire process. Your thoughts and ideas have made this book far better than I could have made it on my own. Your support kept me going as I fatigued. Most of all, thanks for reminding me of something I always seem to forget—that you don't have to do everything in life on your own.

To the very special Mary Burns, I'm not sure where to begin. Thank you so much for your support and guidance throughout this entire process. I am especially grateful for your creative ideas with the book title. I enjoyed our brainstorming session and know your ideas will have a long-lasting influence on the entire series of milewalk Business Books.

To my friends and business colleagues, Jorge Alonso, Tony Aukett, Sam Biardo, Jim Bissing, Joe Condo, Dave Curry, Gerry Holman, Dominic Olson, Jay Simner, and Robert Smith, thanks for letting me bounce ideas during our monthly business get-togethers. A special thanks to Mike Christie. One of your endless little gestures served as a significant catalyst for helping me develop these methods. I will forever cherish your inscribed copy of *Made to Stick* in 2007.

Your words, "Andy, here's to continued success—business and personal!" have served as great inspiration for me.

To my business colleague, Kasey Mueller, our casual lunch a few years ago served as great encouragement. I left feeling inspired, unlike any other time in my professional life. When I'm inspired, I get things done!

To my friend and business colleague, Tricia Tamkin, thanks for helping me see the life I wanted. You served as a true inspiration for me to start milewalk. Without your support, this book would not exist.

To Edward Mack and Mike Scimo, thank you for serving as the only true mentors I've had in my life. As someone who meets thousands of people every year, I marvel at that rarity. It is a tribute to your uniqueness, and I will always treasure your guidance throughout my most formative professional years.

To the folks at Balboa Press, thanks to all involved who have contributed not only to making this book far better than I could have ever imagined, but for keeping me in order throughout the process. Your help with all facets of the book production as well as the press releases, marketing, public relations, and social media activities have contributed to success well beyond the printed product. I'm looking forward to working with you on the next book!

INTRODUCTION

Wise men talk because they have something to say;
fools, because they have to say something.

— PLATO

I'm currently an executive recruiter—haven't always been and might not always be. For the last several years and currently, however, it's what I do every day. Sometimes I even get paid for it. Most people don't understand what executive recruiters do. Candidly, it's not all that important that you do. The only thing that matters is how this book can help you.

Through securing and facilitating thousands of job interviews between companies and their prospective employees, I've observed many idiosyncrasies that contribute to the success or failure of these interviews. Surprising to most, very few of these issues are related to the candidate's job qualifications. In fact, every time a company interviews a candidate, it essentially grants that the prospective employee is qualified. Why else would it take the time to evaluate the candidate?

Even so, most companies, and the people within them, incorrectly assume the vast majority of these recruitment "failures" are due to the candidates being unqualified. Other companies astutely recognize the majority of their recruitment process is comprised of interviewers who are skilled at other functions as opposed to interviewing itself. Often, these untrained interviewers have not become adept at extracting and decoding the information necessary to make sound hiring decisions. They are rarely taught how to effectively sell the organization to the candidates. To further complicate matters, sometimes the true failures are disguised as "successes" because the candidate was hired. These particular situations mask the true problems and simply add to the confusion.

Anyone who has ever participated in a job interview can attest that the process is quite convoluted. I think this is primarily attributed to the fact that people are involved to a great extent. The more reliant we become on human behavior to help solve the issues, the more interference we infuse into the situation—our biases, prejudices, and lack of experience (as well as too much experience) can get in the way. When people are the main factor in the process, there are simply too many variables and potential outcomes to ensure success.

That's where this book comes in. It will help you minimize those variables, as they relate to you and the company, to ensure you achieve the outcome you want—whatever that outcome might be.

Interview Intervention is the inaugural book in a series of milewalk Business Books aimed at helping job-seekers and employers make the most educated decisions regarding their careers and hiring decisions, respectively. While this particular installment tends to focus heavily on the experienced job candidate, first-time employees as well as employers will benefit greatly as most of these principles, especially those centered on interpersonal communication, apply. It is my intent to release subsequent milewalk Business Books more tailored to employers and first-time employees.

Here is a preview of how this book can help:

- Assess your needs to ensure you know the job you want before—not after—the fact.
- Conduct research to surface the most pertinent information related to the employer.
- Address the true reasons you actually get the job.

- Improve your interpersonal communication skills to ensure success during the entire interview process.
- Review the two types of interviewing questions and how to prepare for them.
- Develop a connection with the interviewer to gain the benefit of the doubt.
- Tell compelling, memorable stories.
- Respond successfully to the fourteen most effective interview questions.
- Sell yourself and gather intelligence through question asking.
- Use effective closing techniques to reassure the interviewer and discover the outcome.
- Ensure success when accepting the employment offer.
- Resist the counteroffer temptation.

I hope you enjoy reading this book as much as I've enjoyed sharing it with you. Happy interviewing!

The World Actually Does
Revolve Around You

Research yourself first and the company second.

It seems obvious and easy enough. You're preparing for a job interview with a company, so you'll surf its website, perhaps call a few colleagues, gather some information, and jot down a few questions. You'll be ready. How many times have you thought this?

I'll go out on a limb. You're doing it backward. How do I know? For the last twenty-four years, I've served as a consultant to over 150 companies, helping them improve various business-, technology-, and employment-related issues. For the last seven years, I've focused primarily on executive search activities, helping prominent organizations recruit the best employee talent. In recent years, I've spoken with over one hundred people each week—every week—all year long. Unanimously, they approached changing jobs the same way. I wasn't sure why, because it always seemed illogical to me. They evaluated their available options and chose what they *thought* was best for them at the time. Their first option (if they were employed) was automatically their current job. Good or bad, that current job served as the perennial yardstick until something better surfaced. Their second or third options could have been opportunities they discovered through a job listing, recruiter, employed friend, or some similar means. Regardless of the source, the newly minted candidate likely goes into penciling the advantages and disadvantages of each option, often weighing them against each other. I've even seen some of the more energetic types draw matrices and tables. What I've never witnessed is a candidate who proactively documented or was fully aware of her needs and criteria before she took her first step. These criteria should become the centerpiece against which everything is measured.

As a job candidate, you might think your greatest qualities are your skills, work experience, and bubbly personality. While all are important, I think your greatest asset when evaluating and pursuing a career change is your self-awareness. That self-awareness will help you navigate through the murkiest of recruitment processes and serve as your beacon, especially when you feel that uneasiness in your stomach that indicates something escapable doesn't "feel right." It will also, most importantly, serve as the focal point upon which you can evaluate the company and whether it is right for you.

Throughout this book, I don't define interviewing success as "getting the job." Many candidates who get the job become miserable employees. They might have been better off not getting the job or turning down the employment offer. Success, as I see it, is securing the right job with the right company that keeps you happy for a sustained period. I assume everyone would rather be employed and happy than simply employed. Much of this book focuses on techniques that help you evaluate the company and job as you interview to ensure you make effective decisions regarding your career.

Buy what you need, not what they're selling.

Most candidates I interact with look at their job options in a vacuum that contains only their choice of employers and roles. I have yet to encounter one who, without prompting, has a compelling grasp of "herworkself" and what makes her happy. In my life, for that matter, I seldom come across someone who is self-aware. Some people are satisfied going through life aimlessly, grabbing what comes their way. Others are intent on making things happen. You can go through life in whatever manner you choose, but if you are reading this book, you are likely taking a step toward improving your ability to find or create the right job for you. That makes me happy.

When I open a discussion with a candidate, we talk for a few hours, uncovering a wealth of information before ever discussing her work background. That is because while her qualifications have much to do with her ability to effectively perform her job, her desires and needs have a much greater impact on her overall happiness. Most people look for job opportunities based on what they can do instead of what they want! Why? This seems backward to me, so I never conduct an initial recruiting call based on what someone can do or what her work history looks like. I want to know what she wants to do.

Know what matters to you, before the fact.

I love stories, so you will get a few throughout the book. I would like to open this chapter with one of the more encapsulating events I have encountered while helping match individuals with companies. A colleague of mine who is also a recruiting professional asked me to speak with her husband, who works in the technology sector. Let's call him John to protect the innocent. She shared with me that he is in his early forties and held several jobs throughout his career. She was hoping I could provide some advice regarding how he could more effectively approach his job search. I was happy to do it.

John called, and we got together. I reviewed his résumé, which contained nine different jobs, so he was averaging a couple of years at each company. Early in the conversation, I asked him to summarize in one or two sentences why he held so many jobs.

He said, "Well, the reason for leaving each one is different, so it would be difficult to summarize in one sentence."

I said, "Okay, tell you what. You've already shared with me why you want to leave your current employer. Take me back to your second company and tell me why you transitioned to the third and fourth companies." After he did, I asked, "Do you see the common denominator?" He had a perplexed look.

I said, "John, in each instance, you completely ignored your criteria in favor of your friends' opinions and enjoyment in working at those companies." (In each instance, he was an "employee referral" into the company.) "Let me connect the dots for you. In your current situation, you want to leave for three reasons. First, the company is headquartered in California, and you live here [Chicago]. That doesn't allow for much contact with the senior executives and doesn't help your advancement. Second, you don't support the corporate strategy and the direction the company is headed. Third, you think the software product is subpar. Were you aware of all this before you accepted the position and has anything related to any of these areas changed since you started at the company two years ago?"

He said, "I was aware of those things. The company has always been headquartered in California. The strategy is the same, and I was able to review the software product before I started. So, no, nothing has changed."

I replied, "That's right. All is the same as before you started the job. Do you know the only thing that's actually different between now and before you made your decision to start that job?"

He asked, "What?"

I said, "Now you know those things matter to you."

You need to identify up front what makes you happy (and miserable)—in detail! While this might seem obvious, very few people approach this diligently, feeling comfortable that they know what makes them content as well as what questions to ask a prospective employer to determine whether it would be a good organization for them to work. In fact, most people only become keenly aware of what makes them happy once they don't have it. Most people also don't recognize there is a laundry list of "hard" criteria that affects this; there are also a significant number of emotional influencers as well. These emotional influencers affect your decision-making process when changing jobs and have a greater impact on whether you will leave your current employer in favor of a better overall situation. The next book in this series is a more holistic view of assessing your criteria and the emotional factors that influence not only your job-changing decisions, but also an employer's hiring decisions. For now, I'm including an abridged view for the candidate, so you can be aware of some of the influencers and why they affect you. There are many ways to aggregate your criteria and information against these influencers. While your information can be very lengthy and detailed, I'd suggest grouping it into five key, manageable areas:

- **Current Situation**: Identify all forms of what you currently have
- **Requirements**: Develop a list of your needs and wants
- **Timing Considerations**: Determine whether now is an appropriate time to leave
- **Counteroffer Potential**: Prepare in advance whether you would entertain this
- **Compensation and Benefits**: Review a complete list of your current actual value

Asking yourself the following five questions will help stimulate your thoughts and create a strong roadmap for making sound career decisions. Once you've created this roadmap, you can refer to it throughout the interviewing process to ensure you are staying true to what makes you happy. Remember, it's often better to be slapped with the truth than kissed with a lie. In this case, make sure you're not the one lying to yourself.

Current Situation—What Do I Have?

In assessing your current situation, understand that your current employer will serve as one of the greatest emotional influencers when you change jobs. The company and its people will force you out or keep you in. Understand and review areas such as your relationship with your boss and coworkers. Based on our organization's assessment of over 6,400 candidates, 78 percent cited their boss as one of their top three reasons why they are open to leaving (or have left) their job. There are a few interesting notes related to this statistic. First, it seems to transcend the health of the employment market. During two three-year periods (between 2005 and 2007, a favorable employment market, and 2008 and 2010, an unfavorable market), the percentages were virtually the same. Second, it also seems to be universal across job positions. That is, our company evaluates employees across the entire business spectrum—senior-level executives as well as sales, marketing, human resources, recruiting, finance, accounting, product development, information technology, and various other managerial and junior-level positions. This trend would seem to support the conclusion that people generally quit people before they quit companies.

Even so, the exact opposite also is true as it relates to overstaying. Many individuals are unable to leave their job because of the relationships they've developed with their boss and coworkers. As an executive search firm supporting our clients in securing employee talent, we notice these relationships as one of the single greatest obstacles in extricating employees from their current organization. As such, we evaluate it upfront to determine whether we will face an issue when it is time for the candidate to decide whether to accept our client's offer of employment. You should evaluate this for yourself at the beginning as well. Take a deep look at these relationships and determine in advance whether you will have issues saying good-bye. That alone can save you significant time researching and interviewing with a new company.

Also take a very close look at why you are open to leaving. I call them "wounds," but this can include anything from a minor annoyance to areas you despise about your current job and employer. Are you appreciated? Provided opportunities for career growth? Working with great, smart people? Paid well? Keep in mind, there is absolutely no reason to change companies if you cannot improve the areas you feel are lacking.

Lastly, make sure you have a good handle on all the wonderful things your company and job provide you. While many of these areas will be tangible, such as your compensation or commute, many (if not more) will be indefinable, such as your potential opportunity for growth.

Requirements—What Do I Want?

Make sure you know what you want and what makes you happy. This is your list of requirements. Early in our discussions with candidates, we gather this information, and I refer to it as their Value Package Criteria. This is a holistic view of a person's requirements and how she will evaluate whether the new employer can meet her needs. It is not a matter of whether you are interviewing with a great company. It is a matter of whether you are interviewing with a company that is great for you. In essence, evaluating these criteria will help you determine the overall value the employer can provide to your career and life. After all, a job is far more than simply trading your time for money. These days, work is often integrated into our social lives, and many individuals are working in jobs that blur the lines between work and play. You must evaluate the mixture of what you do, who you do it with, where it is located, how much travel is required, and so forth. It is extremely prudent to highlight all the requirements you have as well as weigh them by order of importance. That will help you objectively determine whether the job opportunity is good for you.

I've mentioned that we have observed over 6,400 employee candidates in the past few years. Based on performing this exercise with each of them, I've determined that—when probed—they favor twelve areas as the greatest influencers of their happiness and longevity with a company. I stress it requires probing, which means you need to allocate an appropriate amount of time to evaluate what truly makes you happy. Otherwise, you risk identifying it only when it is lacking. I have discovered through my line of questioning that most people fatigue after identifying four or five criteria. Therefore, don't be surprised if it takes a few iterations to develop a more complete list. I also suggest speaking with others about what they enjoy (or don't) about their jobs and companies, but keep in mind your list of criteria and its order of importance will be as unique as your fingerprint. These twelve areas cited below, while not intended to be an exhaustive list, could serve as a good starting point.

- **Company Track Record and Position for Growth**. Has the company been growing and does it have a product or service that positions it for future growth?
- **Corporate Culture.** What is the company's "personality"? Is it high-energy, fast-paced, employee-focused, and so forth?
- **Contribution.** Are you in a position to make a significant impact for the company?
- **Appreciation.** Does the company recognize and appreciate its employees' efforts?
- **Role.** Will you be performing interesting, appropriate responsibilities based on your background and capabilities? Can you be successful in the role?

- **Career Development.** Does the organization provide opportunities for you to grow, whether through your daily responsibilities or training classes? Is there an outlined career progression or at least significant growth opportunities for the company, which usually results in opportunities for its employees?
- **Boss.** Will I be working with someone who is smart, supportive, and easy to get along with?
- **People.** Are the employees open, welcoming, and fun? Do they create a team-oriented atmosphere?
- **Office Environment.** Does the office environment induce happiness and energy? Is it architected in a manner that is conducive for successfully performing my job?
- **Office Location.** What is my daily commute? Can I telecommute a few days each week?
- **Travel Requirements.** How much travel is required? Is it domestic and international?
- **Compensation and Benefits.** What is the overall compensation package as well as the health care, 401(k), profit sharing, and additional benefits?

Timing Considerations—Can I Actually Leave Now?

Timing is everything, as the saying goes. I think that much of your success in work or life has more to do with when and how you enter a situation than what you do along the way. Of course, you can make alterations along the way to influence the outcome. I also think that when you quit or leave a situation has an equally paramount influence. Seth Godin's book, *The Dip*, might be a nice reference for those evaluating career choices. It helps you think through whether you are at a dead end or whether you should stay focused and stick with it. This obviously can be helpful in evaluating a job change.

Oftentimes, candidates will engage in opportunities to change jobs without strongly considering the timing elements. On one hand, I preach that your dream job rarely comes along when you're looking for it. (It's probably like love that way.) It would be prudent, however, to fully recognize any timing issues. There are obvious monetary ones, such as when you receive a sales commission check, bonus, or stock option vestment. There are more subtle considerations, however, that people tend to overlook. These could range from upcoming reorganizations with the current employer to your children starting a new school year or your wife delivering your first child.

Keep in mind that many timing considerations can be overcome in a variety of ways. Even so, it is important to be aware of them and evaluate honestly whether they will affect your ability to change jobs.

Counteroffer Potential—Will I Be Tempted to Stay?

Typically, the last item on people's minds as they enter an interviewing process is a counteroffer from their current employer. (This excludes those who seek other job opportunities for the sole purpose of holding their current employer's feet to the fire.) Even so, I suggest you consider whether you have made the commitment to leave your current employer or whether you are "testing the waters." Either is okay, but you should strongly consider the rationale for why you are open to leaving your current company as well as taking the time to interview with other organizations.

I would suggest thinking through whether there is anything your current employer *could* do (not *would* do) to keep you from leaving. If there is anything you can think of, however unrealistic you think it is, I would tactfully approach the appropriate person within the organization to discuss the opportunity. You might think this is corporate suicide. It isn't. If you are in good standing within your company, your employer will likely respect you for thoughtfully expressing your suggestions. One thing that won't go over well is resigning because you have another employment offer.

Compensation and Benefits—What's My Current Annual Financial Value?

Please take stock in what you earn if for no other reason than having a clear picture of what your total annual pot of gold looks like. I genuinely believe that compensation is only one factor in changing jobs, but you should gain a handle on what you earn so you can provide it to the potential employer upfront. I guarantee you will almost never change jobs for the exact same compensation structure. Today, there are entirely too many assets companies can provide their employees. Compensation programs are becoming more complicated, so it might be difficult for you to truly assess the changes. Some of the considerations include your base salary, bonus, stock options, restricted stock units, profit sharing distributions, paid time off, health care and other related insurance programs, flexible spending accounts, and car allowances.

Would you let a twenty-two-year-old choose your career for you—today?

I'd like to include a few remarks for those who are not simply considering a job change but are considering an actual career change. It is not my intent to include What Color Is Your Parachute-type tools to help you discover what might be potential careers based on your interests. I would, however, like to offer some words of encouragement based on my personal experiences as well as those I've witnessed throughout my life regarding career changes.

I was a simple kid from a middle-class Chicago neighborhood. I somehow managed to scratch out an electrical engineering undergraduate degree. The day I threw my hat and tassel in the air, I shut the book on Ohm's law in favor of technology consulting for a firm that was nice enough to give me a job. Somewhere along my seventeen-year technology consulting career, I also managed to open a real estate investment company (which I continue to operate). In 2004, I created milewalk Inc., the executive search firm I currently manage. As I write this, I'm aspiring to become a published author (if you're reading this, I was successful!). I only became an author because I felt I had something to say that might benefit more people than I could personally speak with.

My message in sharing my background is to illustrate that all people have a fork in the road every single day of their lives; every-single-day-they have a choice. Throughout mine, I consciously chose to ignore a few, was completely unaware of some, and took the road never traveled on others. If you keep an open mind, you will see yours.

Life is too short to continue doing something you don't love. Most people I encounter, whatever age they might be, forget that they chose their career at a very young age. Regardless of when you made that choice, you can always change your mind. If you're a young adult, perhaps eighteen or twenty-two years old, entering the workforce for the first time, realize that you can always change careers if you don't enjoy what you're doing. Life is full of wonderful ways to earn a living.

Most people never act on new adventures. It's my opinion that they would rather live with unhappiness than uncertainty. Instead of taking a chance, they hold themselves hostage, with decisions they made during their twenties serving as the shackles. Consequently, they keep plowing forward until they collect their Social Security checks. There are certainly a select few who are fortunate enough to love what they do for their entire careers. Most are not. I'm not sure about you, but I certainly don't want a twenty-two-year-old to pick my career for me—not even a twenty-two-year-old version of me.

Realize the absolute worst scenario in the event you "fail" is to revert back to whatever it was you were doing before you made the attempt. I'm not quite sure who invented the expression, "There's no turning back." Whoever it was, he or she was sorely mistaken when it comes to the workforce. I absolutely guarantee that if you take that new road in the fork and decide it's not for you, the bridge back to wherever you came from will still be there. It might not be with your previous employer, but you will certainly find other suitors in your old field who would welcome you back.

There are entirely too many success stories that support my view. Some individuals who I worked with during my technology consulting career have gone on to prosperous careers as a yoga instructor, chef, restaurateur, woman's retail shop owner, flower shop owner, and photographer. There are countless others that were entrepreneurial enough to open their own businesses in the technology consulting industry. If any of them would have "failed," they could have easily gone back to work in their previous field. If you really aren't enjoying your current line of work or simply aspire to do something else, give it a try!

Corporate information couldn't be easier to find or more difficult to decipher.

Now that you have a good handle on yourself and your current situation, you are better positioned to gather and filter the information to determine whether the company is a good fit for you. While there is still significant homework you can do (more in later chapters), you are much more aware of what to look for as you approach the interview. You can now spend your energy researching the company to gain a better understanding of it.

Our digital age has provided us access to loads of corporate information. Cyberspace is filled with websites, press releases, and other sources, making it easy for you to gather information about a prospective employer. Based on a survey milewalk conducted in

2011, 95 percent of candidates chose the company's website as their first source of information. There is good reason for this. Not only will the employer's site offer significant information, it will also provide a preview into its personality.

While corporate websites seem like an obvious place to start, there are drawbacks. Reviewing these sites will require sifting through loads of content that camouflage the most telling information. We all appreciate remarks such as "our people are important to us" and "lots of opportunities for growth," but candidly I feel these claims simply take up cyber-real estate and provide zero value. Your goal should be to identify information that provides the most relevant insight for you as a prospective employee, especially as it aligns to your Value Package Criteria.

- Why would I want to work there?
- Does the company have a product or service that is valuable?
- Is the company a leader in its industry?
- What is the corporate culture, and is it unique?
- What are the job and career development opportunities?
- Who works there?
- What are the benefits?

Typically, the resources that help answer these questions include videos and testimonials from employees, podcasts, blogs, recruitment newsletters, employee biographies (not only the management team's), and corporate honors and awards.

You will rarely find all this information on a company's website. I suggest reviewing other sites, such as LinkedIn or other socially designed communities, to gather additional information regarding the company's offerings, current employees, alumni, and other pertinent information. Below are some additional sites that contain company information and reviews. Keep in mind, people who contribute to some of these sites are current or former employees whose experiences will differ.

Glassdoor is a company and salary research site. It provides a community for job seekers to review and monitor company insight, ratings, salaries, management team approval ratings, competitors, and other general corporate information.

Vault Career Intelligence is another source for company reviews. This site provides job seekers with information on over ten thousand companies. This site also provides guides (for a fee) as well as videos related to interview dos and don'ts. Much of the information you need is free, but you can pay a fee for additional information you feel worth it.

WetFeet is a site filled with job-seeking advice, blogs, guides, and other career development-related information. The company-specific information is high-level but will serve as a nice supplement to whatever you have already reviewed. You can purchase reference material a la carte or subscribe for other services.

If the organization is publicly held, you can review its annual (10K) and quarterly (10Q) reports, which are usually filled with rich content. These reports will likely serve as a stimulus for great questions and can typically be found on the company's website or the United States Securities and Exchange Commission website (Edgar). If the organization is privately held, review sites such as Hoover's, which provides insight, analysis, and financial information for companies and industries.

Here's my nickel's worth of free advice.

If, either before or after your interview, you choose to gather additional information beyond your online findings, I caution you to approach it carefully. I'm speaking of discussing the opportunity with coworkers, colleagues, family, or friends. Gathering insight from these people might seem prudent, but you will likely be seeking counsel as well as listening with one of the most common prejudices—the confirmation bias. The confirmation bias is a cognitive issue in which people tend to seek sources and favor information that confirms their preconceptions or desires.

The bias itself is manifested from the time you start gathering information. Experiments have shown that individuals are selective in who they seek guidance (or evidence) from as well as how they phrase questions or slant information. They look for results they would expect or, in this case, want. Often while job changing, they provide tailored information to their "counselors" so those individuals are more inclined to validate the candidate's preference. This leads to the proverbial "tell me what I want to hear." This becomes an even greater concern when discussing the job offer, but it can be equally detrimental at the beginning and throughout the recruiting process, because you position yourself toward a self-fulfilling prophecy. My suggestion would be to do enough homework to become knowledgeable about the company, but enter each interview without leaning one way or another. An open mind will serve you best.

Behind the Scenes—
An Insider's View

Your qualifications get you the interview. Beyond that,
they have very little to do with getting you the job.

The truth is once you secure the interview, your job qualifications and fit for the company have very little to do with whether you are offered the job or not. Realize, if you have already secured the interview, through either your own means or someone else's, the hiring company has essentially granted that you have qualifications worth evaluating. So what happens between the time you begin your first interview and the company's decision whether or not to hire you? People speak to each other.

There are three reasons you actually get the job.
Unfortunately, you can only control one of them.

Based on my observation from thousands of interviews between my clients (the hiring companies) and candidates (prospective employees), I have concluded that a candidate's attainment of the job is largely contingent on three often undetectable success factors:

- The candidate's ability to effectively articulate her qualifications and potential contributions (encoding)
- The interviewer's ability to accurately interpret the candidate's qualifications (decoding)

- The interviewer's capacity to remember the candidate (memory)

The reality is the candidate has a greater chance of failing the interview because of a misrepresentation or misinterpretation than she does a lack of qualification. Therefore, as a candidate, one of your main goals during the interview should be to effectively articulate your value to ensure the interviewer understands it. In turn, you need to ensure that you accurately interpret the interviewer and company's offerings.

Can you hear me now?

It might be easier to think of the first two issues, which require interpretations, by another name—communication gaps. Essentially, I refer to these gaps as encoding and decoding issues on the speaker and listener's parts, respectively. The candidate's role will obviously change from one to the other, as will the interviewer's, throughout the discussion. Why do these gaps occur? Let's review how this works in general. As communicators, we speak and listen with a certain bias that was formed from our perspectives of life, a particular situation, work history, and so forth. These biases are somewhat similar to the previously mentioned confirmation biases, but they are more systemic in nature. As a result, we often miss essential information about what others think or how they perceive our actions. This can be further exacerbated if either party does not accurately articulate what they think.

During your interview, you have knowledge of what you've accomplished, experiences you've gained, what you're trying to communicate, and how the interviewer's actions appear to you. You don't, however, fully understand the interviewer's needs or how you appear to her. As a result, you only have half the information necessary to accurately interpret the situation. The situation is made worse when neither of you are aware of it. Instead of recognizing these gaps, you fill them with your own assumptions. This occurs naturally, leaving neither person feeling the need to clarify or question their reasoning or understanding. The most unfortunate part is that the candidate bears the greater burden of ensuring that neither misunderstands what is communicated (because theoretically the employer is the party with something to offer).

They won't forget how you make them feel.
And they'll use two adjectives to remember it.

Your ability to influence the interviewer so she has a positive, favorable memory of you plays just as key a part in your interviewing success (albeit during the aftermath) as your ability to accurately interpret each other. There are two critical elements of importance related to her memory. The first occurs during the interview, as you plant the memory, and the second is related to how she later recalls it.

During your interview, the interviewer is simultaneously interpreting your comments and projecting your potential contributions and long-term fit within the organization. Her interpretations tend to be based on how she "feels" about you. You know who she thinks fits well in her organization? Someone she likes. This always brings to mind one of my favorite quotes by Carl Buechner, who said, "They may forget what you said, but they will never forget how you made them feel."

Obviously, it is paramount that you impress the interviewer to elicit a positive reaction and feeling at that moment, but it is equally important to ensure she can recall it later. Why? Because an employer's hiring decision simply does not happen in "real time." Often, companies are meeting days or weeks later to determine which candidate to hire. Sometimes, in the worst and all-too-often cases, a human resources or recruiting official is chasing an interviewer a week or more later to gather her feedback from your interview. You need the interviewer to give you a thumbs-up. What now? You need her to remember that she "felt" you would be a great employee. Since your interview, she has interviewed three other candidates and has worked several projects amidst a host of meetings, working overtime, and navigating through a number of other "urgent" matters. How will she remember you?

Let me share some insight regarding how her memory works. There are many factors that influence memory, including the emotional charge (your first child), mood (stressed or anxious), distraction (am I prepared for that next meeting), age, and so forth. In addition to those emotional influences, there is the ever-present Forgetting Curve. Hermann Ebbinghaus, the German psychologist, conducted a well-known study that highlighted the pace at which we forget. In short, he showed the exponential decline in how quickly humans forget, with the sharpest decline occurring in the first twenty minutes, followed by the next largest within the first hour, before the leveling off occurs after one day.

Assuming the interviewer is now required to access her long-term memory, most of which is depleted, she can do that in one of two ways—recognition or recall. Think of recognition as a means of remembering through multiple choice options and feelings of familiarity (e.g., I've seen that face before). Recall, on the other hand, requires her to proactively search her memory on her own. As you can imagine, this requires much greater effort.

We have all had to do this before, so it is easy to believe that she would want to store information so she can retrieve it with as little energy as possible. Regardless of when the memory occurred, she will not be able to recall it with much detail. Instead, as psychologist Daniel Gilbert points out in his book *Stumbling on Happiness*, her brain has recorded the seemingly necessary details and will fill in the rest when it is time to remember. Essentially, she did not store your discussion in her memory in its entirety. Rather, she compressed it down to summary phrases ("short, red hair" or "great candidate"). Later, when she needs to recall the experience, her brain will quickly reengineer the memory, not by actually retrieving it, but by fabricating most of the information. This occurs so effortlessly that she will have the false impression that it was in her head the entire time.

You now need the interviewer to recall those summaries of you. You want her to remember phrases such as "positive energy," "detail-oriented," "articulate," "knew the technology," "implemented it before," and "team player." I assure you she will not remember the details of why she thinks this, but she will definitely remember these impressions. I can certainly attest to thousands of interview debriefs I've conducted with clients, who relay how they felt about the candidate but are unable to explain in detail to me why that is. Sometimes these calls occur mere hours after the interview.

For now, simply be aware of these critical, unseen success factors related to interpretation and memory. In subsequent chapters, I'll review how to position yourself to enhance your communication, minimize the misinterpretations, and plant favorable impressions through effective storytelling and questioning.

The Two Types of Questions

I want to know what you did or what you will do.

If you have done research on yourself, the company, and perhaps the interviewer, you essentially have what I refer to as static intelligence. It is the information you use to create your game plan. You start to think about which questions might come and which questions you should ask. (I will spend an entire chapter on the latter.) I love planning, but I think the most effective plans not only have backup plans, they also leave enough room to take forks in the road and go with the flow. As former heavyweight champion Mike Tyson once said, "Everyone has a plan til they get punched in the mouth." I gather some interviews may have felt like that, but I think the smartest, most effective and creative candidates do not get rattled because they know how to adapt whenever they encounter something unique or "off book."

The good news for you is that I genuinely believe there are only two types of questions an interviewer can ask. They are "What did you do . . . ?" and "What would you do . . . ?" That is it. Every question, however disguised, can be classified into one of those two categories. Once you recognize the question type, you can formulate your response accordingly to ensure the interviewer develops an accurate picture of your viewpoints and capabilities. Why is it important to understand the type of question? So you can overcome one of the most common communication gaps in any interview. I'll share more on this later.

Please tell me what I need to know, not what I ask for.

When an interviewer asks a "What did you do?" type of question, she wants you to relive what you said or did in the past so she can determine whether you possess what she considers the requisite skills, personality, or traits to succeed within her organization. If the majority of her questions are of this variety, it is a good indication she thinks your past experiences will be a strong indicator of whether you will be successful.

When an interviewer asks a "What would you do?" type of question, she wants you to simulate how you would approach and execute the scenario or problem she posed. Oftentimes, she will identify a real-life business issue the company has faced. (Sometimes, you will get the oddball fictitious situation. In that case, the interviewer is more interested in evaluating your overall thought process.) If the majority of her questions are of this variety, it is an indication she trusts your work history and is more interested in evaluating your potential capabilities.

The interviewer's ultimate goal, irrespective of approach, is to determine how you will perform within her organization. Some employers favor the historical approach ("What did you do?"), believing that past behaviors and experiences are great predictors of future behaviors. Many employ the Critical Behavioral Interviewing (CBI) concepts, which have been around for decades. (You can do a Google search for information related to CBI and easily find the most commonly asked questions and suggested responses.) Others favor a more simulated approach ("What would you do?"), arguing that addressing real-life scenarios you are likely to encounter are a better indicator. Some companies approach the process from both angles, which is the technique I favor.

The list below shows ways interviewers can disguise a question, even though ultimately every one will fall into either category. This should help you identify the question type during the interview.

"What did you do?"

- Tell me about yourself.
- Why did you leave your most recent company?
- What do you know about our company?
- Why should we hire you as opposed to someone else?
- Can you tell me about a time when [insert any Critical Behavioral Question here]?
- Can you tell me about your Rolodex?
- What is your management style?

"What would you do?"

- Why would you leave your current organization?
- Why would you want to work here?
- What would be your next ideal position?
- How long will it take you to get up to speed or make a contribution?
- Describe your ideal boss. What would your ideal boss look like?
- What would you improve about your current company or job?
- What's the first thing you would do if we hired you?

Why is it important to be able to determine the question type? It will help put you in a position to overcome the most common communication gap in any interview. Before we address that, let's review some of the issues you will need to overcome in the interview and why the communication gap occurs in the first place. Keep in mind, the vast majority of interviewers are untrained in either technique and, even worse, are ill equipped to accurately predict your success based on your responses (even if they are correct). Remember, you are often sitting across the table from someone who has a full-time noninterviewing job, just like you. Typically, the company threw that person in front you, perhaps with a list of questions, but more likely she is simply winging it. And the interviewer is likely to spend merely an hour with you.

Where does that leave you as the candidate? Well, at least it is helpful simply to understand the situation. This will put you in the right frame of mind to actually help her overcome her individual lack of experience and training as an interviewer or limitations with the overall process. Ultimately, you want to leave her with an accurate, favorable impression of you.

The communication gap typically results from an interviewer's imbalance of the two techniques, which leaves her with insufficient information to determine whether you can actually perform well in the job. Typically, the interviewer's line of questioning falls short of gathering enough evidence because she becomes overly reliant on the simulation questions ("What would you do?") and never follows through with "What did you actually do?"

My years as a recruiter have been filled with many feedback sessions from clients who explain, "Your candidate provided all the right answers when I asked her how she *would* do it, but I'm still not sure she can do the job effectively." This is usually followed by my question, "What makes you think that?" The client typically responds, "Because she didn't indicate any times during her career in which she actually did it." My response, of course, is, "Did you ask her?"

You get the picture. The interviewer drew a conclusion based on a lack of information that resulted from a lack of effective questioning. (Your inability to read her mind didn't help.) So what should you do to avoid this situation? Make sure to provide the interviewer with an opportunity to gather information from your historical experience. You can eliminate the gap simply by following your remarks to a "What would you do?" question with a question such as, "Mr. Interviewer, I hope that provides you with a good idea of how I would handle that situation. Would you be interested in discussing a scenario in my past where I actually encountered that situation (or a similar one)?"

"Friending" the Interviewer

*The fastest way to develop a connection with
the interviewer is to shrink the world.*

People buy from who they like. Most are even willing to pay more for the comfort level. Companies are no different. They hire who they like. They hire who they know. They hire friends of who they know, and so forth. Your first objective in an interview immediately following the word "hello" should be to shrink the world. One of the easiest ways to do this with the interviewer is to find your commonalities or connections. I recommend doing it as early in the interview as possible to gain maximum benefit from it.

Once you are able to establish your commonalities, the interviewer's demeanor might become more welcoming or relaxed. More importantly, the interviewer will start to fill her communication gaps with positive, rather than negative, assumptions regarding you. In effect, you have altered the interviewer's biases and likely will start gaining the benefit of the doubt rather than receiving the more often present detriment of the doubt.

How do you find these commonalities? A few clicks around the Web is the easiest way. You will likely uncover common colleagues or friends. Professional networking or social media sites such as LinkedIn and Facebook are wonderful tools. With the onset of social media, there is a high probability you will find some valuable information. Sixty-five percent of online adults use social networking sites, according to Jobvite, a California-based software company that specializes in recruitment. Their 2011 study, *The 33 Essential Recruiting Statistics,* highlights this and other relevant information.

Shrinking the world is the fastest way, but sharing
the same passions might be the most effective.

While having a personal connection through colleagues can create a nice bond, sharing the same interests might create an even greater one. Sharing the same experiences builds a kindred spirit that figuratively says, "I understand you." This is typically a bit more difficult to identify early on, because an interview process would rarely start here. You can, however, be observant and glance around the interviewer's office to see if there are books, pictures, plaques, objects, or other trinkets that expose the person's interests. Comment if you think it is appropriate.

Another effective technique is to "cast your line." Early in the conversation, insert comments about your interests and passions. How you introduce yourself and speak about yourself matters. If you integrate facts and interests into your stories, you will provide the interviewer opportunities to connect. That is also one of the most effective ways to create a picture for the interviewer, as I'll discuss in later chapters.

Regardless of the technique you use, be sure to let the interview unfold naturally as opposed to being obvious that you are fishing for some common interests.

Interviewers are dog lovers too.

This is true for everyone but especially the nervous types. There is absolutely no reason to be anxious during an interview. The maximum "punishment" is you do not get the job. Last time I checked, anyone interviewing for a job didn't have the job yet anyway, so technically you didn't lose anything other than a bit of your time. (Technically, you gained an experience and insight about yourself, the company, and its people, so you are likely ahead from the encounter.)

One of the easiest ways to relax those worries is to remember you are interviewing with a human who has hobbies and interests. Interviewers are marathoners, fisherman, golfers, parents, siblings, and a host of other things. You might have gathered clues to those interests if you noticed pictures or surrounding trinkets in the office using the techniques cited earlier. One of my favorite "common interest" stories occurred with a reluctant client. I recognize this is not 100 percent analogous to interviewing for a job, but this story centers on woman who would determine my company's fate regarding supporting her organization, so I think the magnitude is sufficiently in line and hope you roll with me on this one.

A senior executive from a prominent software firm in Chicago called me based on a referral from another client. This executive needed recruiting assistance after a few unsuccessful attempts with other search firms. I went to his office to discuss his requirements. The next day, after a little homework on both sides, we had agreed to terms. He asked me to follow up with Global Director of Recruiting to ensure we executed the contract properly. She offered me twenty minutes of her time, so I went to meet her. I was out of her office in eighteen minutes.

Over the next month, she was relatively evasive to my calls. I'm not sure why, and it doesn't matter. One morning, she and I were on the phone, and my dog uncharacteristically barked (I worked from home at that time). I said, "Sorry about that. I think my dog got excited about something." She asked, "You have a dog? What kind? I have three. They're my life." This was followed by fifteen minutes of chit chat about the dogs. We were e-mailing each other pictures. You get the gist. From that moment, our entire relationship changed and evolved into one of the most successful professional relationships in the history of my firm. To this day, I would call her a friend.

You won't know a person's interests until they surface. In this case, it was by accident. In the case of your interviews, recognize that you can make your own luck by remaining observant.

For the really clever, you can give yourself a head start.

In addition to operating a recruiting firm, I am part owner and an advisory board member of an agency called 7Summits. We help our clients create and implement social business strategies. The company was named after the highest mountain summits on the seven continents—to represent our team's resourcefulness and ability to reach a goal. My search firm also supports its recruiting activities.

Speaking of resourcefulness—the CEO is a charismatic man named Paul Stillmank. He loves hiking, fly fishing, and photography. Anyone can surf the Internet to discover this with very little effort. One clever individual decided to take it a bit further. Paul called me and mentioned he recently received a box in the mail. He said, "When I opened it, I saw one hiking boot. There was a card included, so I obviously opened it." He opened it to find this letter:

> Mr. Stillmank, I have my boot in the door. Now I just need to get my foot in it. This boot has been to the top of four of the seven summits. Please accept my résumé for your review. I am extremely passionate about social media . . .

Is this gesture a bit over the top? Maybe. What is not in question is its relevance. It was also an extremely creative way to ensure he surfaced his credentials to arguably the most important person in the organization. It also demonstrated passion on the candidate's part. While it remains to be seen whether we will hire this individual, one thing is certain—he will receive a call back, something that absolutely must happen in order for him to get the job.

Storytelling

Say it so they get it. Say it so they remember it. Say it so they want it.

That phrase is simple. Remembering those eighteen words, which ought to be easy enough because most of them are the same, at a minimum provides you with a successful formula for the interview. (Don't worry that in twenty minutes you won't remember them. You can always highlight the line with a marker or use the nifty highlight feature if you're reading this on an e-reader.) Until now, we've discussed some key techniques for preparing as well as exposed the critical factors for interviewing success. You are aware that your success hinges largely on your ability to accurately articulate your qualifications and fit for the organization as well as become a timeless memory for the interviewer. So how do you do that? It starts with your stories.

Make yourself sticky.

How do you get them to accurately interpret your comments and remember you as a great candidate? In 2007, brothers Chip and Dan Heath released a book called *Made to Stick*, with the byline highlighting why some ideas survive and others die. It is a fascinating book that reviews why some stories are memorable and others are not. I think everyone in the advertising field should have a copy of this book on her desk.

The book walks you through examples of selling a product or reliving stories for friends and highlights techniques to grab and keep people's attention so they are alert, interested, and engaged. As I read the book, I started thinking about how these concepts applied to interviewing. There is no question you are selling yourself in the interview, so the analogy was an easy one to make. Because I believe that the requisites for a successful interview start with a clear understanding and creating a memorable, positive impression, I started using some of their conclusions as pointers when preparing candidates for interviews.

In summary, they determined through exhaustive research that "sticky ideas" had six key qualities. They were simple, unexpected, concrete, credible, emotional, and story-like. It seemed obvious to me. If a candidate wanted to convey an accurate picture of herself, engage the interviewer, and become memorable (in a good light, hopefully), she should structure her responses in a similar manner. This has become the central theme for me as a coach to the candidates as well as employers—I want to teach them *how* to say what they want to say, as opposed to teaching them *what* to say.

While I've used their conclusions and six qualities as a starting point for these techniques, I've realigned and refocused them in a manner that is more appropriate for interviewing purposes:

- Keep It Short and Simple. Superfluous information hinders their ability to remember.
- Capture and Keep Their Attention. They can't remember you if they're not listening.
- Talk in Their Lingo. Speak in a language they understand.
- Make Them Believe You. Use details to make yourself believable.
- Get Them to Care. Highlight the benefit to the individual in addition to the company.

- Get Them to Act. Engage the interviewer to play along and act on your behalf.

Keep It Short and Simple

Antoine de Saint Exupéry once said, "Perfection is achieved, not when there is nothing more to add, but when there is nothing left to take away." Candidates would be wise to take note. There is a big difference between providing a clean, thorough answer and babbling on forever. Your goal should be to highlight the most necessary information your interviewer seeks without including superfluous remarks. The presence of unnecessary information has two harmful effects. First, you are asking the interviewer to wade through your response to find the information she needs. Second, even if you made nothing but brilliant points, you are asking her to retain much more information than she needs. It not only exhausts her, but you also run the risk of her considering you obnoxiously verbose. It simply makes it harder for her to remember you as someone who "knew his stuff" versus someone who was "obnoxiously long-winded."

I am not suggesting being overly brief to the point she isn't getting a complete picture of you. I am recommending you do it in pieces so she can more easily digest the information and request when she wants more.

Capture and Keep Their Attention

"Unexpectedness" was the term Chip and Dan Heath used. They determined there should be a means of surpassing people's expectations and being counterintuitive. Doing this with the element of surprise would not have long-lasting effects, but interest and curiosity would.

This particular quality, in my opinion, confronts one of the greatest hurdles you will likely encounter in any communication—

getting people's attention. If you think for one second that you have the interviewer's attention, you are sorely mistaken. Let's see, she has a meeting immediately following your interview. She is not quite fully prepared for it. She is not sure how she is going to explain to her client that the project is delayed. Her Crackberry keeps ringing. The instant messaging chat keeps beeping. All of this is happening as you are sitting in front her (imagine what she is doing if you're on a phone interview). You get the picture.

There are two main issues here. The first difficult obstacle is that you cannot make her pay attention. You need to attract it. Once you get her attention, you need to keep it. The easiest way to capture someone's attention is to break a pattern. If an individual is anticipating what you are about to say, she generally tunes out. If, for example, you are a technologist interviewing with another technologist, that person likely has the benefit of similar experience (or perhaps more aptly termed "Curse of Knowledge"). She runs a greater risk of tuning out because she is familiar with what you are saying, likely has experienced it herself, and is hearing what she expects you to say. If you started speaking Swahili in the middle of your response, she would likely immediately notice it. To be effective in grabbing her attention, you need to eliminate the predictable, break her chain of thought, and then fix it for her. That will get her attention.

The easiest way to break a person's pattern and grab her attention is to surprise her or make her think she's about to be surprised. Either way, she will notice you. Once you have her attention, the easiest way to hold it is to keep her curious.

This is often much easier to do than it might sound. Here's a simple, nonprofessional example related to grabbing attention. The other day, I was at the health club at an extremely early hour. I was in the weight room with two other people, neither of whom I knew by name. I recognized one, as I see him virtually every time I'm there. We nodded to each other and I asked, "How are you doing this morning?" I anticipated him saying, "Good. And you?" or something similar. He replied, "So far, so good." So simple, but not what I expected. I smiled and replied back, "That'd usually be a great accomplishment for me too, even at six o'clock on a Saturday morning." I still don't know his name, but I won't forget his response, which indicated that he's probably an interesting guy.

You're probably wondering how to do this during a run-of-the-mill interview, where you're providing matter-of-fact responses. There are certainly many ways to do this, but I think these three techniques should suffice in most situations: 1) doing it first, 2) doing it wrong, or 3) confirming their guess. (Keep in mind, doing it better, while effective, won't break their pattern. It might get them to remember you did it well, but for our purposes, we want to make sure she is actually listening to you.) Let's use the technologist example above to discuss these three techniques. I think these illustrations can be used regardless of the situation. Simply align them for your purposes.

When doing it first, you become a pioneer. People love pioneers, because they often have information they are unaware of. She will anticipate something she's likely to learn. The technologist could sprinkle phrases into the discussion such as, "As I was designing the system, I used a technique that had never been implemented before. I'll share it with you now to get your thoughts." This will keep her attention throughout the story, because she will want to know what you thought, what you did, and how it ended.

Doing it wrong doesn't need to create negative connotations. Often, we can use these techniques to highlight how we learned and grew as a result of it. Candidly, mistakes and failures are necessary for your professional and personal evolution. You can use this technique with phrases such as, "I realized as I was designing the solution that I was about to make a grave mistake. At first I was going to . . . and then I realized . . . and then discovered the best technique would be to . . . This taught me so much about these new technologies." She will be anchored on your discovery, how you cited it, what you learned from it, and how it helped you grow.

Sometimes you simply don't have a change-of-pattern item at your disposal. Your story is generally consistent with what she would anticipate, so you want to tell it as cleanly and quickly as possible. In that case, you can confirm her guess and grab her attention by using phrases that make her think she might be surprised. Toss in a few, ". . . so I was designing the solution with the usual hardware and software including . . . you might be thinking it would yield these results. I did too. But then I checked these other angles to ensure it would work properly. Fortunately, in the end, it did produce the results you and I anticipated." Keep in mind, you don't have to knock a person over or play the scary, suspenseful music in the background to grab their attention. A simple nudge now and then will make sure the interviewer is alert.

Talk in Their Lingo

Pick your expression. Put it in their terms. Target your audience. Speak in their language. You get the picture. Realize that interviewers are busy, and many have likely been placed in front of you out of obligation. They are untrained and might be assessing you strictly for cultural fit or something "softer" than your job-specific capabilities. It might be because they are unable to comprehend what you're capable of, or they might simply be breaking apart the process to evaluate you from many sides. Regardless of the reason, you need to adjust your responses so they understand and remember them.

In my opinion, this is one of the most difficult things for people to do when they're communicating. Do you know why? Because as we evolve through life, we forget what it's like not to know what we know. Here's a little story for you. I have a battery of exercise trainers and medical professionals that keep me tuned for life and the kamikaze sporting events I love. During our training sessions, my trainer has a habit of saying things to me like, "Your gluteus maximus isn't engaging quickly enough, which puts more pressure on your gastrocnemius and soleus muscles to keep the lower part of your leg and ankle stable while your foot pronates. That's why your posterior tibial tendon is swollen and your navicular bone is dropping." I'm thinking, "Huh?" You can imagine I'd like to throw my high school biology book at her when she says something like this to me. Obviously, that's not a friendly response, so typically I simply laugh because she is doing what most people do when they communicate to someone else—anyone else—communicate as if your audience was you.

As you prepare for your interviews, you need to think about what it is like to be the interviewer. Keep in mind, a professional title is not always a dead giveaway of what a person knows or has experienced, but it can serve as a starting point. (I also recommend doing thorough reconnaissance on the interviewer if you are aware of her name. Use sites such as LinkedIn to gather a more complete profile of what she does and where she's worked.) Regardless of her title, you can use a few techniques to determine what language she actually speaks. First, you can simply ask her the level of information that would be appropriate. You can also pay close attention to the depth and content of her questions. Questions from a human resources official related to what you're looking for in your next role can be answered at one level. Questions from a technologist who wants to understand specifically how you would design software might be answered at another. If the verbal cues are missing, you can always looks for squinted faces, dropped eyebrows, or lack of eye contact as a cue that the interviewer doesn't understand you.

Ultimately, if you can speak in a manner that allows the interviewer to literally visualize what you're describing, you've mastered speaking at the appropriate level. This means you have found the common denominator around which you can both communicate. It likely means you are using specific nomenclature that helps her comprehend how you felt, what you built, and so forth.

Make Them Believe You

In all honesty, telling stories that are believable is probably one of the easier obstacles you need to overcome. The reason is that if you truly lived the event you're sharing, you have the specific details that will help them believe you lived it. Making them believe you provides the interviewer with two of the most important qualities about you—sincerity and experience.

Regardless of the interviewer's adeptness at interviewing, she is a human being. Humans can smell dishonesty a mile away. It has a certain undeniable stench to it. Your level of genuineness, on the other hand, is something that will remain consistent throughout the recruitment process (assuming that the process is thorough enough). Experience is a critical component they seek. Is the candidate actually qualified? Does she have the skills and experience to succeed in the job?

While there are many ways to get someone to believe you, there are essentially two means for our purposes. First, you can provide an external authority to vouch for you. The more trusted the resource is to the employer, the more weight her opinion will carry. This technique is often used when a company is conducting a formal reference check, an informal reference check, or an employee referral to validate your previous experience and performance. This avenue is obviously something that you cannot control and, while helpful, should not serve as your sole method to reinforce your credibility.

The more direct and controllable technique is to smother the interviewer with details and use statistics if appropriate. Your goal in the interview is to gain internal credibility, which can be validated through external credible resources such as your references. To clarify, when I refer to details, I do not mean being verbose and violating our first principle of remaining brief. I am suggesting sprinkling in specific information about how you designed something, solved an issue, managed a project, or sold a product. Sharing with the interviewer a step-by-step process will make her feel as though you actually lived the situation and therefore have the experience she is looking for. I also recommend highlighting only the details that actually matter to the situation.

An excellent supplement to the details is statistics. I would add precise statistics. For example, your interviewer might be interested in whether you had a sales quota last year and how you fared against that quota. She would be far more inclined to believe you if you indicated your quota was $1 million and you exceeded it by $257,000 than if you said you exceeded it by approximately 25 percent. If your project took fourteen weeks to complete, indicate the project took fourteen weeks as opposed to approximately a quarter of a year. Employees who have earned significant accomplishments simply remember them because of the amount of time they took to achieve and their level of importance.

Get Them to Care

While believability might be easy to attain, getting them to care might be more difficult. This is true for two reasons. First and foremost, you will not be her top priority at that moment. The interviewer might grant you full attention in rare cases, but more likely her focus will zoom in and out intermittently, thanks to the breakneck pace she works at. Unfortunately, you are her midday distraction. Second, I believe people are generally good-hearted and willing to help in most cases, but my twenty-five years of corporate experience has shown me that the overwhelming majority of the workforce operates with their self-interests in mind. So how do you get them to care?

The next words I'm about to write pain me. The easiest way to get the interviewer to care is to show her how hiring you benefits her (or something she cares about). Sure, she will care how hiring you benefits the company overall, but often the specific impact to her will carry more weight. I'm guessing some will think otherwise, but subconsciously, this is a factor for most interviewers.

Tactically, you need to highlight how your capabilities and contributions will impact her. There are different techniques you can use, depending on where the interviewer works in the organization. If you are interviewing with a superior, for example, you might indicate that if you were hired, your skills are strong enough to help relieve her of some of her daily duties so she can focus on more strategic areas. When speaking with a peer, show how you could serve as another resource to share ideas and cross-train each other on your complementary skills. To a subordinate, you could highlight the areas in which you can teach or mentor her and your desire to present her with challenging opportunities for growth. These are just a few examples to get you thinking about the possibilities. These points can be worked into your responses to many commonly asked interviewing questions such as "Why should we hire you as opposed to someone else?" "What unique value do you bring to the organization?" "Can you provide examples of how you are a team player?" and "How would your team members describe you?" This will become much easier if you have prepared and given thought to the key attributes you want to highlight. As you can see, there will be many opportunities if you are ready for them.

In addition, you can also take advantage of this technique when it is your opportunity to ask questions. One of the more potent interviewing questions I suggest for my candidates is to focus on the benefit for the interviewer. For example, you could ask, "If you were to present me with a job offer and I was to accept, what would be the first activity or project I could do to make your life easier?" That question applies irrespective of whether the interviewer will be your boss, peer, or subordinate. With that simple question, you have personalized your connection to the interviewer and showed her that you care about how hiring you benefits her. It might sound subtle, but I assure you the impact will be significant.

Get Them to Act

If you strip it down completely, your ultimate goal in an interview is to get the next interview or job offer (whichever the case may be, depending on where you are in the process). To focus on anything else is simply distracting yourself. Let me clarify. At any moment during the interview, you can only focus on one thing (contrary to what a multitasker thinks): selling yourself in an accurate light. This should occur when responding to the interviewer's questions *and* when asking your own questions (more on this in a later chapter). Each moment is a building block for accumulating enough good will to move to the next step. I realize there are many additional components to the interview, such as learning more about the interviewer and the company. That is true, but you eventually want the option to work there, which means you don't want them stopping your journey prematurely. If you reach the end of the recruiting process and the employer presents you with a job offer and you still have outstanding questions, you can continue asking them until you feel you've gathered the complete picture.

It boils down to her giving you a positive review and encouraging the company to hire you. How do you ensure she does this?

It required no effort on your part to get her to care about herself. That was innate. You simply connected the dots for her to realize how hiring you benefits her. Getting her to act on your behalf is a different story, one that you now face. You simply need to remember that people exert energy for those they like—consider this stage a culmination of all the good will you've built from the time you started the interview until now. People act when they feel emotional about something. If you have succeeded in all the previous steps we've discussed, she will feel emotionally positive about you because you showed up on time, were well prepared, looked put together, "friended" her, told compelling stories, and convinced her how she benefits from hiring you.

My "Silver Bullet" Interview

How you say what you say is just as important as what you say.

As you read this chapter, I hope you take note I did not title it the "The Most Common Job Interview Questions" or "The Best Responses to Interview Questions." There are many good books that identify common interview questions and acceptable responses. There are, in fact, as many good (and bad) answers to every interviewing question as there are people in the workforce. I am not, however, a fan of providing overly scripted responses. I think that is akin to a doctor giving me ibuprofen to treat a serious ailment.

The main goal of this book is to educate you on how to perform well in any interview, irrespective of the questions posed. The insight within should transcend interview questions, interviewer styles, or job sought. In that spirit, it is my intent to stimulate ideas for your responses by creating awareness of the interviewer's intent along with critical areas she wants to evaluate. If you understand these underlying principles and recognize the interviewer's intention with each question, you will put yourself in a much better position to provide effective responses and perform well.

One way to illustrate this is by using interview questions as examples to build on the principles we have discussed thus far. Through these examples, I will identify the area, trait, or skill the interviewer is attempting to evaluate. Since we are going to use these interview questions as a vehicle to discuss this, I thought it would be beneficial to cover what I consider the most effective interview questions. Let's call it my version of the "interviewer's silver bullet list" because I think these questions elicit the maximum amount of information in the least number of questions. Keep in mind, this list is intended to cover all professions and omits any industry, role, or domain-specific experience that might be relevant for your particular job. Those questions would be supplemental. Lastly, to lend most credibility to the sample responses, I generally leaned toward the technology sector because it is the industry with which I am most familiar. I think, however, that you will find the overall structure general enough to apply to your profession.

These fourteen questions and their variations, if executed correctly, will provide the interviewer with an accurate picture of you. I refer to the first four as "Pillar Questions." Every interviewer, at some point in the session, will be interested in this information regardless of whether she asks these four questions directly. The best interviewers typically ask them in this order, right at the beginning of the interview.

1) Why would you leave your current company?

Areas of evaluation: What are the candidate's current pain points; is the candidate a malcontent; how plausible is it the candidate will leave current employer; can the company provide the candidate a better opportunity?

In my opinion, this is one of the best openers because it provides the interviewer with loads of information regarding you. It highlights how you feel about your current employer, role, and situation, as well as surfaces your pain points. The interviewer can begin to evaluate early on whether her company can actually address that pain and truly offer you a better situation. It also helps her identify whether you will be realistic or practical in your needs.

Other variations of this question that address these same issues include "Why did you leave your current company?" and "Take me through your job transitions throughout your career."

Regardless of whether you are actively or passively seeking a new job, it is paramount you provide insight that shows you would leave for the right opportunity. At the same time, it is crucial you avoid portraying yourself as a malcontent; do not badmouth your current employer. While this might seem obvious, many of us become unaware of the undercurrent in our tones or comments when speaking about something as important and emotional.

The easiest and most effective way to balance the plausibility and malcontent components is to speak only about issues that you do not hold your employer responsible for nor can alter through your own actions. The interviewer will consider you tactful and professional if you avoid sounding disgruntled, but it is also important not to complain about something you could actually change. This, in fact, is one of the greatest mistakes a candidate can make early in the interview. Below are a few examples to illustrate this.

Candidate: "I would be open to leaving my current employer for a position with more challenging career development opportunities."

While this sounds neutral, the interviewer could infer that you are not performing well enough for your employer to challenge you with more rewarding opportunities or that you are not taking responsibility for proactively growing yourself professionally. Furthermore, what would prevent you from leaving them for another company that provided you a better opportunity? (An effective interviewer would likely follow your response with a question asking you how you are addressing this issue currently.) During the interview, it is irrelevant if neither of those thoughts are true. *The only point that matters is what she thinks.* Sadly, in many cases, there is often a communication gap between what you said and what she heard. Remember, your goal is not only to sell yourself and your value, but also do it in a manner that leaves no room for misinterpretation. Whenever you encounter an interviewer continually asking additional questions about your original point, you can be fairly certain she is unclear of your intentions (not necessarily your response) or there is a communication gap.

An alternate, more effective way to handle this particular reason might highlight certifications you have recently achieved or areas of interest. For example:

> *Candidate:* "I would be open to leaving my current employer because we are not in a position to secure opportunities for me to work in an area that greatly interests me. Recently, I attained [insert certification here] certification with the hope of working in that area, but my organization has decided to hold off providing that service to our customers. It is an area of great interest to me, and I'm hoping to leverage my learning from that certification process. The primary reason I'm interviewing with your company is because that area is one of your core services and appears to be a large part of the job responsibilities."

In the latter example, the candidate remained neutral regarding her employer (i.e., the company made a conscious decision regarding which services to provide its customers), and she took action to further her career development. You have also provided the interviewer a preview into the next question she will likely ask.

2) Why do you want to join our company?

Areas of evaluation: How passionate is the candidate about the opportunity; has the candidate performed extensive research; what does the candidate know about the organization; can the company provide the candidate a better opportunity?

This question and several others like it (e.g., "What do you know about us?" "What do you know about the role?" and "What have you heard about our organization?") are aimed at evaluating two key areas. First, the employer is gauging your level of research. This shows how interested you are in their organization and job opportunity. Second, they are assessing whether they can actually provide you with a better opportunity than your current employer.

Your most effective response will show you have done your homework and know specific areas the employer does well. Hopefully, you can also highlight how these areas match your interests. The ultimate answer will illustrate how the potential employer can satisfy interests your current company cannot.

This response could be lengthy, based on how many areas you want to address. Here is an example that would include specific information and provide the interviewer with a sense of your range of research.

Candidate: "My research shows you are the leader in your space because you've developed a product and service that [insert detail here]. It is extremely important for me to work in an organization that prides itself on being a leader and is willing to invest in developing unique products and services. I read in *Forbes* magazine that your company invested $100 million in research and development to ensure the product contained next-generation features that no other company's included. Another aspect that intrigues me is that your organization is multinational. I read in Hoovers that 30 percent of your revenue comes from outside the United States. My organization focuses exclusively in the United States, so my current responsibilities are exclusively national. One of my criteria for professional growth in my next position is to gain international experience. I noticed from the job description that international travel is part of the job. I also reviewed the backgrounds of your employees [name an employee here for specificity] and noticed your people have incredibly strong backgrounds. It is important for me to work with smart, accomplished professionals because I feel that will help me grow as well. I also noticed the testimonials they provided highlighted how much they enjoy working here. I drew the conclusion from those videos that the organizational truly supports its workers."

3) What value do you offer?

Areas of evaluation: Can the candidate sell herself; does the candidate have unique skills; does the candidate have an understanding of the company and job responsibilities?

This question is rather generic and broad and could come in many different forms, such as "Why would we hire you instead of someone else?" "What makes you unique?" and "What special skills do you have?" I love this question because it helps the interviewer understand what you *think* your strengths are. Of course, simply because you say you have the skills does not necessarily mean you actually have them, but you are putting the interviewer in a good position to probe in those areas. You can also provide evidence that you have the skills to preempt a series of questions.

There is a shortcoming with this question. For the interviewer to elicit the most substantive information, the candidate must understand the job responsibilities. In the event this question comes at the beginning of the interviewer, I would recommend that you gain clarification before responding. If you simply start answering her question, you risk highlighting unique skills that are irrelevant for that position. (I consider this a poor tactic on the interviewer's part because without clarification upfront, you will likely waste precious interview minutes providing insight that is not as valuable.)

Instead, use one of the most effective sales techniques—sell the customer what she wants.

If the interviewer asks this question, simply respond, "I would be happy to discuss the value I can bring as well as unique skills I possess. First, can you let me know which specific areas of the job responsibilities are most important to you so I can focus on my skills as they relate to those responsibilities?" This will put you in a position to highlight areas the employer feels are the most important.

When responding, it is important to not only indicate your unique skills but also provide evidence of where you attained them. For example:

> *Candidate*: "I have a unique ability to sell services within a complex sale. Last year, I was able to secure nine new clients for the company, which generated $10.7 million in consulting services. In five of those cases, we were invited to respond to a Request for a Proposal and won. In the other four situations, I showed the prospects business issues that were present but latent. Because these issues were yet unknown to the management teams, I was able to work with them without our competitors present. I showed them how my organization could solve the issues as well as the potential return on investment. I had become a trusted advisor so those prospects did not feel the need to seek competitive bids. As a result, we were able to secure those clients and have now expanded throughout the organizations, providing other services we offer."

4) How will you benefit from joining our company?

Areas of evaluation: Can we actually provide the candidate a better opportunity; does the candidate already see how we provide a better opportunity?

Other variations of this question include "How will you improve yourself within this job?" and "What can we offer you that another company cannot?" This question is designed to determine whether the employer truly can offer you a better situation than you currently have.

This question is aimed at determining whether it would be a smart career move for you to join their organization. It also reinforces the likelihood that you would join if they provided you an employment offer. As with the previous question, it is important that you are detailed in your response. I have recycled a portion of the example I used for the response to "Why do you want to join our company?" because of its applicability.

Candidate: "One of the key reasons is that I would gain multinational experience. I read in Hoovers that 30 percent of your revenue comes from outside the United States. My organization focuses exclusively in the United States, so my current responsibilities are exclusively national. One of my criteria for professional growth in my next position is to gain international experience. I noticed from the job description that international travel is part of the job."

5) What is the first act you'll perform when you start?

Areas of evaluation: Does the candidate have a good understanding of the position; will the candidate get up to speed quickly; will the candidate be able to make contributions quickly?

Other variations of this question include "How do you envision your first thirty (or sixty, and ninety) days on the job?" and "What do you know about the position?" Regarding the last example, I favor my originally cited question because it essentially conflates the two (i.e., what do you know and what will you do when you start?).

This question is designed to evaluate how much you know about the company and position as well as simulate how you would approach your initial days working for the company. Does the candidate have a good understanding of the position? Do I need to share more information with her? Is she organized in her thinking and approach? How effective are her organizational skills?

An effective response to this question will include a confirmation of your understanding of the position followed by a list of your assumptions and completed with a thoughtful, organized approach, including specific details regarding what you will do. Below is an abbreviated example for a sales position.

Candidate: "I'd like to confirm my understanding that this sales position primarily focuses on securing new accounts from a provided list of targeted customers (as opposed to determining who I need to target or growing accounts from an existing customer base). If that is the case, I would forego any market research, at least upfront, required to determine which customers to target because I will focus on the list you provide.

"During my initial week, I assume I will either undergo training the company provides or educate myself on the products, services, and the company's approach to selling them. Once I've completed orientation process, I'll align my network and relationships to the targeted list of customers to determine the overlap. I should be able to complete that assessment by the end of the second week I'm on the job. After that exercise, I will prepare a detailed thirty-, sixty-, and ninety-day schedule based on the jumpstart my relationships will provide. That will allow me to either create suitable metrics including number of phone calls, meetings, proposals, and so forth or help me determine my work pace based on any expectations and metrics you have in place."

Obviously, there will be a significant content difference depending on the position for which you are interviewing, but the important points to note are that the candidate is providing a response that shows the interviewer a number of positive things. First, the candidate immediately introduces opportunities for the interviewer to clarify any incorrect assumptions. Second, the candidate is demonstrating that she knows how to execute sound sales processes, is metrics-driven, and has an organized, planned approach to how she will operate her day. Even if some of her assumptions are incorrect, the interviewer is able to gather the essentials she needs to make an accurate assessment of the candidate's longer term potential.

6) If you were still working here three years from now, what do you think your most significant contribution would be?

Areas of evaluation: What is important to the candidate; does the candidate have a realistic view of what she can accomplish; is the candidate a creative thinker; does the candidate have practical work experience that can help her formulate ideas and execute them; can the candidate set and execute on goals?

As much as I love this question, I want interviewers to avoid questions like "Where do you see yourself in five years." I understand they want to gain insight into your ambitions and desires for the future, but most people can't see past tomorrow, let alone five years from now. Furthermore, today's job market changes so quickly that new opportunities are created on a daily basis, and career paths are changed in an instant. If someone would have told me in 2003 that I'd be opening a recruiting firm the following year, I would have bet my entire bank account against it. I honestly wish someone could dis-invent that question or somehow permanently remove it from every interviewer's repertoire of questions.

This question is designed to evaluate whether you are goal-oriented, a planner, and an executer. The best response will be similar to how Harry reads a book in the movie *When Harry Met Sally*. When he starts a new book, he actually reads the last page of the book in the event he dies before he finishes it—so at least he knows how it ended. A little morbid, I know, but effective during this type of question. You want to tell the interviewer the result and follow it up with how you would accomplish it. For example:

Candidate: "Three years from now I would expect that I helped build for you a successful video practice with approximately $3 million in consulting revenue. During the first ninety days, I would begin identifying, developing, and packaging the solution offerings. Based on my current experience with these products, I already have strong ideas that I would want to obviously discuss and confirm with your management team to ensure they align with your corporate direction and strategy. Once we agreed and built the offerings, we would start developing the marketing campaigns, educating and supporting the sales teams, and identifying the appropriate product development and professional services resources to support the implementations for our customers. Based on our first year's results, we would plan the targets for year two. I already have completed market research for the demand for these solutions so I have a good idea of the potential customer base. That would help prepare realistic targets . . ."

You can see the candidate first provided a direct response. Most importantly, she followed up with a mixture of evidence that shows how her experience and exposure to the market has placed her in a good position to make immediate contributions as well as ensure the company can set and meet its goals by executing a well-thought-out plan.

7) Describe a situation when you and a coworker (superior, peer, or subordinate) disagreed. Take me through the disagreement and how you discussed your viewpoint.

Areas of evaluation: Does the candidate have strong interpersonal flexibility skills; will the candidate get along with team members; is the candidate influential; is the candidate accommodating; can she compromise when appropriate?

Other variations include "Tell me about a time when you needed to influence a coworker" and "Describe a situation where you needed to plead your case to a coworker."

I have a news flash for you. The best influencers in the world are not salespeople, slick-talking politicians, public speakers, or anyone else of that ilk. The best accommodators are not the spineless types or the best team players. People that can get along with others and have strong leadership and influencing skills all have two things in common—*they are the greatest listeners* and *they are inquisitive.*

Here's why. The fastest way to influence someone or come to a compromise is to accommodate their need in a manner they think is best for them. The only way you're able to do this is if you understand what their need is or where their viewpoint comes from. Impressing your viewpoints upon them will accomplish nothing if they are not receptive to other options or do not see the benefit for themselves.

I always tell people during discussions like this, "It matters more to me why you think what you think than what you think. Whether you are correct or not isn't as relevant to me when I'm trying to help you. I need to understand why that's important to you or why you think that or where you got your information."

For anyone in the workforce, you will become a lot more influential if you learn the following lesson quickly. In business, it makes no difference what is correct. It matters far more what is practical and has the greater return on investment. Whenever you are evaluating, discussing, brainstorming, or whatever exercise you're in the midst of, remember there exist political, social, economical, government regulatory, competitive (product features, price matching, etc.), and a host of other factors that ultimately influence the best solution. This holds true whether you work in a restaurant or a skyscraper.

When responding to these types of questions during an interview, you would be best served to explain to the interviewer that you have a particular philosophy whenever you disagree with someone. That philosophy should be to seek first to understand the other party's viewpoint and why she thinks that, including many of the internal or external influences. (If this is not your normal inclination, I suggest you think back to situations when you were more apt to do this and cite that example in your response.) Once you are able to do that, you can focus on compromising or providing additional viewpoints, knowing much more information regarding why it is important to them.

8) Describe an ambiguous situation that you organized, resolved, or executed.

Areas of evaluation: Does the candidate have strong organizational skills; is the candidate a self-starter in assembling the components necessary to bring order?

Other variations of this question include "Describe a situation where you solved or implemented something you considered complex," "Describe a situation when you took initiative on a project," and "Describe a situation where you implemented something without being asked."

This is a relatively straightforward question regarding what the employer ultimately seeks. The interviewer wants to understand whether you can operate independently in an organized fashion. The most important element in responding to the question is to ensure you can find a rich example where you identified the necessary components or activities that needed to be executed in order to complete the product, project, or group of activities.

When responding, be sure to include how you started, how you executed, and how you ended. It will be easier for the interviewer to follow along and remember your story if it is figuratively outlined for her—*start, execute, and finish.* Alternatively, you can think in terms of architecting, implementing, and operating (or whatever else might be appropriate for your field). You can handle the critical success factor of "making them believe you" by iterating details within each of the sections of your response. For example, below is a marketing executive who is attempting to identify the best approach for a marketing campaign:

> *Candidate*: We needed to execute a marketing campaign and wanted to isolate it to one of our customer segments because we didn't have the budget to cover accommodations for all three (top, mid, and low) levels of customers. We also didn't have enough data to determine which customer level would be most effective to target. [She identified the problem and highlighted the ambiguity.] To be successful, I knew I first needed to gather the analytics to determine which group to target. Second, once I had that information, I determined what the campaign should be based on the customer level. I then built the material and distributed it. After the campaign was executed, I monitored the activity using our sales force tracking tool to assess the level of performance of the campaign based on the number of responses and leads we incurred."

The candidate can then revert back to the beginning to highlight the details of each phase to show the interviewer her logic behind the approach, the thoroughness of the execution, and how she captured and monitored the results. The interviewer won't necessarily remember any of the details, but she will remember the candidate had a logical approach and a detailed understanding of the process.

9) Describe a situation where something went wrong.

Areas of evaluation: Does the candidate respond well to adversity; is the candidate composed in stressful situations?

Other variations of this question include "Describe a situation where you faced a conflict" and "Describe a situation where you failed."

This question is designed to determine whether you can rise above conflict and how you address adversity. A key ingredient to your response is to describe how you remained calm when you initially discovered the unfortunate turn of events. Reinforce how you recognize that mistakes, failures, and other unfortunate situations are part of growing as a company and an employee.

Once you lay the foundation with those thoughts, you can articulate the entire situation. The ultimate responses will also include how you prepared for these types of situations in advance by identifying potential risks, mitigating plans, and contingency plans in the event something goes wrong.

Below is a rather simple example for a candidate who was providing a sales presentation to a prospect:

Candidate: "I went to a prospect to deliver our final sales presentation for a sizable deal we were pursuing. The prospect indicated they would provide the necessary audio and visual equipment for the presentation, including a video machine to project the presentation onto their boardroom screen. I arrived a bit early to set up. When I got to the boardroom, the receptionist shared with me that the video projector bulbs had burned out that morning and they didn't have an alternate machine. I wasn't overly concerned because the previous day I spent a few minutes considering and planning for all the meeting requirements that were out of my control. The equipment was just one of them, so I anticipated something like this could occur. Before I left the office, I made hardcopies of the presentation just in case. The prospect was very appreciative and one of the individuals indicated it was a plus that I had a contingency plan. Interestingly, that unfortunate situation presented an opportunity for me to score additional points that I wouldn't have had the opportunity to if something didn't go wrong."

10) How do you educate yourself?

Areas of evaluation: Is the candidate resourceful; is the candidate a self-starter; is the candidate interested in continually growing professionally?

Other variations include "How do you further your career development" and "Tell me about the last time you took initiative to learn something that was not part of your job description."

This question is designed to reveal whether the candidate has the desire to grow professionally. I think this speaks to an individual's level of motivation, but it also focuses on the candidate's resourcefulness and creativity in how to learn.

The best responses to this type of question will highlight the numerous, specific sources you would seek for the information. While you can rely on teammates to help educate and cross-train you, employers are usually more interested in the sources you would deploy on your own. Typical references would include the Internet (be specific as to the sites or genres), books, trade magazines, workshops, additional schooling, training classes, and so forth. The more specific your references, the more they will like your response.

It is also effective to lay out the sequence in which you'd review this material. That is, you won't examine all the information from all sources simultaneously, so review which source you would approach first (because it is likely to have the richest and most relevant information), second, and third. Below is an example:

> *Candidate*: "I have encountered numerous situations where I needed to educate myself because I didn't yet have the requisite experience. I usually put together a short workplan for myself, highlighting what I consider to be the most robust sources of information and sequencing them based on quantity of information I'll be able to extract. To ensure I'm starting in the right location, I usually review the plan with my boss or the appropriate individual. While I don't like to consume too much of his or her time educating me, having them review the plan for a few minutes often times saves a lot of time for me. Then I start with . . ."

11) How would your coworkers describe you?

> *Areas of evaluation: How does the candidate view herself; what does the candidate consider her strengths and opportunities for improvement?*

Other variations include "What would your coworkers (or others) say about you?" and "What would your boss, coworker, or subordinates consider your greatest strengths/weaknesses?"

This question is designed to reveal how you view yourself. It is often asked in place of the one related to your greatest strengths and weaknesses. I recommend that you provide only positive remarks regarding how your coworkers would describe you. That is a completely fair response on your part. I'm smiling as I write this because, let's face it, if the interviewer wants you to discuss your weaknesses, make her ask for them specifically!

The best responses to this type of question will cover your greatest strengths. It is certainly all right to provide only these. In my opinion, the question itself is a bit unfair because it is asking you to speculate. I'm not in the speculating business. I'm in the success business, and you are too.

12) What motivates you?

Areas of evaluation: Is the candidate self-motivated; are the candidate's interests in alignment with our offerings and needs?

This question usually stands alone, but employers have also been known to explore outside your work-related motivations. For example, the interviewer might ask, "What motivates you outside the workplace?" to gain an understanding of your hobbies or interests.

This question is designed to determine whether you are a motivated individual in general as well as whether your interests are in alignment with the company's needs. Obviously, it is not an effective match if you are interested in areas you would not have an opportunity to work in or that the company could not provide. This leaves two things to consider before responding. First, determine whether you have a good understanding of the position, and then highlight your motivations as they relate to the role (and potential future roles if you know those career options also exist). If the interviewer asks this question before you have strong understanding of the role, simply ask a clarifying question to ensure you can calibrate your answer. For example:

> *Candidate*: "I have many motivations and interests related to my work life. Would it be most beneficial to highlight the ones most closely aligned to the role? [If she indicates no, then go directly with your motivations in general

and use your best assessment of the role to match them. If she indicates yes, then continue with the following question.] Then can you share a little bit more about the main responsibilities so I can provide you an accurate picture?"

You might be hesitant to answer a question with a question. I don't consider this evasive unless you continually follow up with question after question. If you can show the interviewer that you are trying to help her get the most relevant information in the shortest amount of time, she will appreciate that. Using pointed follow-up questions such as the one cited in the example will help you acknowledge that you want to answer the question directly. It will also ensure you are providing the most pertinent information to help the interviewer assess you.

13) Do you prefer working on a team or by yourself?

Areas of evaluation: Is the candidate a team player; can the candidate work independently?

Other variations of this question include "Tell about a time when you sacrificed meeting your deadline in favor of helping a team member" and "Describe how you are a team player."

This question is designed to determine whether you are a team player and whether you can operate autonomously. When an interviewer asks this question, she is usually trying to assess whether you play nice with others. This is often a critical success factor in most environments, but not in every one. You can determine what is appropriate based on the position you are seeking.

If you are pursuing a position that requires significant team interaction, there are several qualities that you might want to highlight in your response. Typically, the most effective team players listen well and are helpful, are open to others' ideas, are mentors, are nonjudgmental, and are willing to sacrifice their own well-being or praise for the good of the group. There are a number of appropriate ways to communicate this. The most important factor in an effective response is that you must show how you possess that quality. Simply saying you listen well or are open to others' ideas will not convince the interviewer. Below is an example:

> *Candidate*: "I was working on a team and our project was due in two weeks. While my components were going well, there was an individual on the team who was falling behind because she had less experience and wasn't as knowledgeable about our software product. I know how that feels. We all have to be beginners at some point. Recognizing this, I decided to stop working on my components and help her exclusively until she was able to complete her work. I was aware this would require me to work a significant amount of overtime during the weekend, but I was willing to make that sacrifice because the product would not function properly without her piece of the software, and we would not otherwise achieve our release date."

14) Describe your ideal boss.

Areas of evaluation: Does the candidate fit well with her potential boss; what type of people does the candidate get along with; will the candidate require or want extensive supervision?

Other variations of this question include "What did you love about your favorite boss?" and "What do you not like about your current boss?"

I think this is a fantastic question for many reasons. First, I mentioned previously (and will mention again, because I never want you to forget it) that a significant percentage of job quitters leave because of a poor relationship with their boss. If that's the case, why wouldn't an employer ask you this question? I'm actually quite baffled when they don't. (The same goes for the candidate when given the opportunity to ask questions.) Second, it will provide the interviewer insight as to whether you want (or don't want) or need (or don't need) a micromanager.

Before we review what to do, let's review what not to do. Do not, unless expressly asked, comment on what you don't like about your current or former bosses. You might think it sounds silly that I consciously pointed this out. The reason it is important for you not to fall into this trap is because quite often it is easier to describe what you want by sharing what you don't want. When I interview candidates and ask them to cite their needs (their Value Package Criteria), an estimated 40 percent want to brainstorm based on what they don't want. (I always attribute to this to the fact that negative—and recent—emotions carry more memory and weight.) For example, "I don't want a micromanager" or "I don't want to be locked in an office for forty hours every week" and so on. Remember, speaking about the positive qualities and what you actually want not only will present a more accurate picture, it will actually elicit a more positive response from the interviewer.

Stay focused on all the good qualities you want in a boss (or people, for that matter). Some of the greatest bosses and leaders are individuals who provide support, trust, mentorship, coaching, autonomy, freedom, and other means to allow the employee to grow. Here is one of my favorite quotes from Timothy Ferriss, writer of many books, including *The 4-Hour Workweek*: "It's amazing how someone's IQ seems to double as soon as you give them responsibility and indicate that you trust them." Some people might want to be motivated out of fear, but most prefer nurturing and support. Whichever qualities you seek in a boss, highlight the positive traits and leave negative ones alone.

Profit from Questioning—
Sell Twice, Buy Once

*In an interview, waste no time doing anything that
doesn't help sell you—not even when asking questions.*

When preparing candidates for their interviews, I often ask them
whether they have started planning questions. I also want to
understand what they consider the main purpose of asking questions.
The typical response is, "So I can gather information to make a
good decision about whether this is a good company and place for
me to work." That, in part, is true. In my opinion, however, that
only covers one third of your opportunity.

Bear in mind, when the interviewer asks, "Do you have any
questions?" she has literally given you control of the interview.
Why focus solely on gathering intelligence? You certainly don't
have to follow her script, at least for the time being. You now get
to say and ask anything you want! Take it—own it.

If I can't see it, it must not be true.

I'll help maximize your benefit of asking questions a bit later in
the chapter. First, I'd like you to think back to the interviewer's
perception, interpretation, and memory issues related to your
remarks during the interview. Keep in mind that these issues are
ever-present, so you will also need to account for them when

preparing for and asking your questions. Most of what I have reviewed thus far related to those issues has been oriented toward verbal communication. That is only part of the equation. You must also account for interpretations drawn through your nonverbal actions. Never, during the entire interview, are you more susceptible to nonverbal miscues than when asking your questions.

I once had a senior-level information technology candidate interview with my client for a chief information officer position. He successfully navigated through several rounds of interviewing, and we were preparing for his final interview with the chief executive officer. The senior vice president of human resources explained that this was more of a formality than anything else. The CEO simply wanted to meet the candidate to ensure there were no glaring issues that the rest of the staff overlooked. (At this point, I was practically spending my recruitment fee on the new car I wanted. This would help me upgrade the model!) After the interview, the candidate called to inform me that it went well and he was excited about the opportunity. Great! The next day, the SVP of HR called to let me know they were passing on the candidate. He said that the CEO felt the candidate was unprepared for the interview. Specifically, he indicated the candidate was "winging it" when given the opportunity to ask questions. The candidate apparently had no notes or portfolio of documented questions. The candidate appeared to act as though he felt that this meeting was not important, and he seemed ill-prepared. I called the candidate to relay the feedback. When I asked the candidate whether this was true, he replied, "I had a few dozen questions prepared for the CEO. I asked him most of them and was able to obtain the information I needed." I asked, "Did you have them front and center so he could see the level of work you put into preparing them—like we discussed?" The candidate said, "Well, no, I had them memorized." Insert buzzer sound here. Now you don't have a job offer. It's not what you do or say, it's what they see and hear.

This is one of the easiest ways to score points in the interview before you utter a single word. Lay out your research, notes, and questions in front of you. I encourage the candidates to highlight with various colors, underline, sticky-note-tab, or whatever other means to help them organize it. Unless the interviewer avoids all eye contact with you, she will notice that you have put thought and energy into it. This shows you did your homework.

There are obviously several additional nonverbal cues to proactively address. Make sure to be on time, bring copies of your résumé, prepare sample material if applicable, dress appropriately, comb your hair, shine your shoes, and so forth. All these little things help.

The way you organize your questions can help you reanswer the interview questions without saying a word.

I love free stuff. I don't care what it is. I'll take whatever anyone wants to give me. If I don't enjoy it, I'll pass it to someone else who might. As you prepare for your interviews, I suggest subscribing to this philosophy. That is, position yourself to realize maximum benefit with the least amount of effort—take these free opportunities along the way to sell yourself. The way in which you organize your questions is one way to accomplish this. In addition, the technique in which you ask your questions can save time, thereby maximizing the number of questions you can ask and the amount of information you can gather.

By organizing your questions into one of three buckets— Company, Role, and Boss—you can maintain a prearranged flow of information for the interviewer and also sell yourself in the process. (While I would generally reserve the boss-related questions for your potential boss, you could substitute more appropriate interviewer-centric questions for any interviewer that would not be your boss. See the last section in this chapter for examples.) I'm convinced any question you can imagine will fall into one of these three categories. Furthermore, this provides you with a manageable number of groupings to access and review for each interviewer.

1. *Company*: Includes questions aimed at surfacing corporate-level information. These questions could be related to financial health, revenue, earnings, organizational structure, employee base, corporate strategy, market position, products, services, competitors, management team, and corporate communications.

2. *Role*: Includes questions related to your specific job. These questions could be related to your typical responsibilities, team structure, performance review process, career development opportunities, and career path.

3. *Boss*: Includes questions related to your potential boss. These questions could be related to your boss's management style, expectations, and plans for the future.

The sequence in which you ask the questions also plays a significant part. Asking company-specific questions at the beginning serves two purposes. First, it provides the most essential information you need about the employer. Remember, you join a company—you do not join a job. If you pick the right company, you don't have the job you started in for very long. I mean that in a good way. The most successful companies are continually growing their people. The role you are interviewing for is a mere entry point. Second, it shows the interviewer you are a team player, big-picture-thinker, unselfish, organized (for your entire approach to questioning), and a host more. You have instantly reinforced your answers to the interviewing questions she likely asked twenty minutes prior. She is now gaining additional insight to her questions such as, "Describe how you are a team player," "Tell me about am ambiguous situation that you organized," and so forth. Free stuff!

Conversely, asking role-related questions first can actually have an adverse affect, for the same reasons. If you focus immediately on the role, the interviewer could misconstrue you as self-centered or more concerned about yourself than the company or team. While this might not be true, you want to avoid opportunities for her to misunderstand. Focus on the organization first and follow up with questions related to the job. This will help you gather insight regarding your immediate responsibilities, which will help you determine whether you can be successful initially. Most companies will insert interviewers early in the process who possess detailed knowledge of the role you are interviewing. This helps you understand the position and helps the employer sell the company.

Follow the company and role questions with those regarding your potential boss. Four out of five people quit their jobs because of their boss (have I mentioned this before?). I suspect this statistic will remain constant forever because people simply quit people before they quit companies. Gaining insight into your boss's management style and expectations will help you determine whether this individual will be supportive and provide you opportunities to growth.

Let's feed three birds with the same piece of bread.

I don't like killing things, so let's use that more inspirational expression instead of knocking birds out of the sky. Now that you understand an effective outline for grouping your questions, you need to prepare for one of the most important aspects of the interview—your specific questions.

I often tell candidates there are many rich opportunities to sell yourself once you gain control of the interview. By developing and asking great questions, in the proper way, you can deliver the knockout punch. You ultimately get the chance to make two sales and a purchase simultaneously with every question—you have an opportunity to show how passionate you are, demonstrate how smart you are, and gather intelligence. That intelligence should be used for short-term and long-term purposes, as I'll discuss later. I refer to those three benefits as the Triad to Asking Questions. In addition, you can tack on a host of other subtle niceties related to demonstrating your organizational, research, and preparation skills.

Before we discuss the specific structure to questions, it is worth noting that this is the part of the interview where the candidate is at greatest risk of wasting time, because the interviewer is not always providing the information the candidate needs. This is rarely attributed to the interviewer and more often a result of poor questioning on the candidate's part. That is, the candidate leaves too much room for interpretation for the interviewer. The interviewer, in turn, provides information that might be interesting but not as valuable to the candidate. As you structure each question, you can avoid this situation and realize all benefits by focusing on the triad:

Passion: Show strong interest in the company, role, and interviewer. The easiest way to show your excitement is to overtly mention the research you performed.

Smarts: Demonstrate your level of expertise and intellect. The most effective way to illustrate this is by asking astute questions that require the interviewer to think as opposed to answering your questions with simple facts.

Intelligence: Gather information you actually need to help you determine whether the company is a good fit for you. The most straightforward means to elicit this information is to inform the interviewer specifically why you want to know.

Let's review an example of two candidates to illustrate the point. The first candidate, a senior executive, is interviewing with a human resources executive for a technology consulting firm. The second candidate is a professional services software developer interviewing with the same HR executive. Both decide to ask the same question, but for two entirely different reasons: "Can you please describe your client portfolio?"

The senior executive is interested in whether there is a sufficient balance between industries and clients to ensure the company remains healthy in the event a significant client leaves or there is an economic downturn in one of the industry sectors. The software developer wants to understand the different types of clients and their locations because she is interested in understanding which sectors she'll be supporting and where she will likely travel. How will the interviewer know how to answer the question? Rarely will the interviewer clarify the question with a response such as, "Why is that important to you?" More often, she will simply start speaking and provide superfluous information the candidate finds unimportant for her needs or decision process. Consequently, much time is wasted. Instead, I would encourage you to maximize the three benefits and position the interviewer in advance to narrow her response so she can address your most pertinent needs. For example:

Senior Executive: "I was reviewing your annual report for 2010 and noticed that your client portfolio included 25 percent of your revenue with financial services firms, 33 percent with healthcare organizations, 10 percent with manufacturing companies, and 32 percent with public sector institutions. Now that we are approaching the end of 2011, I'm interested in understanding the current balance for this year since you have yet to release that information publicly. The reason this information is important to me is that I want to ensure the organization remains balanced for stability purposes. I am also curious as to whether you are planning to focus on any particular sectors for 2012 because I have more experience in some than others."

Software Developer: "I was reviewing your annual report for 2010 and noticed that your client portfolio included 25 percent of your revenue with financial services firms, 33 percent with healthcare organizations, 10 percent with manufacturing companies, and 32 percent with public sector institutions. Now that we are approaching the end of 2011, I'm interested in understanding the current balance for this year since you have yet to release that information publicly. The reason this information is important to me is that I want to understand the types of companies I will consult for because I have more experience implementing solutions in some sectors than others. That will also provide me with a sense of where I'm likely to travel."

In both examples, the senior executive and software developer highlighted the research they performed (showing passion, interest, and exerted energy), asked an intelligent question that they could not find the answer to themselves, and directed the interviewer so she could focus on their respective areas of interest. This will not only ensure they're gathering their most pertinent information but also increase their opportunity to ask additional questions by eliminating wasted time. The more intelligence they can gather, the more educated their decisions will be.

While there are several variations you can use to ask effective questions, the following generic example might serve as a good starting point to assemble your questions:

Candidate: "I was reviewing [insert reference material here—could be from the employer's website, public reports, magazine articles, TV, etc.] and noticed [insert relevant astute observation here]. I'd like to know [insert well thought out question here]. The reason I'd like to understand that is [insert specific rationale here]."

Once I have the information I need, how will I use it?

You have the outline (Company, Role, and Boss) as well as the technique to structure the questions. There is one last question you need to ask yourself before you begin preparing your specific questions: How will I use the information? I tend to look at questions based not only on how I will use the information, but also when I will use the information. During your interview, you will be extracting information for either a short-term or long-term purpose (or both). I consider questions yielding a short-term benefit if you can use the information either immediately or throughout the interview process to sell yourself. I consider questions yielding long-term benefit if you need to ponder the information to determine whether the company is a good fit for you. Let's take a look at a few examples:

> *Short-Term/Role-Related*: "I reviewed all of the employee testimonials and videos on your website and thought the individuals within your company are quite intelligent, energetic, and passionate. None of those employees, however, were in the unit for which I'm interviewing. I was wondering whether you could share what you consider the qualities and characteristics of the most successful individuals on that team. The reason I'd like to understand this is to ensure that I would fit well with my potential teammates."

The interviewer will now highlight those characteristics for the candidate. The candidate, in turn, can make notations of these qualities, which are essentially what the company wants to duplicate and hire. The candidate now knows the type of person the company seeks and can use this information during that interview as well as subsequent interviews to craft responses that illustrate how she possesses those qualities.

Long-Term/Role-Related: "I reviewed the job description and made additional notations based on your assessment of the role. In addition, I reviewed your website and LinkedIn to see whether I could get a good sense of the organization structure. I'm sure I don't have a complete picture, so I'd like to get a more detailed understanding of that as it relates to the career development and long-term job opportunities I might have. The reason I'd like to understand this is because there are a few areas which interest me, and I want to determine whether I would be putting myself in a position to realize that a few years from now."

The interviewer will now highlight the potential career opportunities beyond the first job. The candidate can make notations and determine whether she is positioning herself for long-term growth. While we all know there are no guarantees in life, she is at least gathering some of the possibilities and can consider this when she evaluates a more complete picture of the company and career move.

I can tell far more about a person by the
questions she asks than the answers she gives.

There are many great questions you can ask to elicit information to help you determine whether the company is a good fit for you. Identifying and shaping the questions that are specific and most beneficial for you will likely depend on your Value Package Criteria (i.e., your needs and interests you outlined when reviewing yourself), the type of company you're interviewing with, the potential position, and your experience level in the field.

I've included below a few of my favorites as they relate to each of the categories. This is by no means a complete list, and you can certainly tailor them for your appropriate use. I've omitted the prelude (of research) and trailer (your rationale for wanting to know) components, as those will be specific to you. Lastly, you want to make sure to avoid asking questions that you can easily find the answers to yourself. It is entirely too easy these days to use the web to research information that can help you. Employers know this. Stay clear of asking questions that you can easily track down, otherwise the employer might consider you lazy.

Company

- Can you provide insight into the overall company structure? It would also be helpful to understand the management team structure, revenue, and number of employees in each of the areas.
- Based on the company's position in the market, what do you see ahead for the company in the next few years? How do you see the overall performance for the company's target market or industry? Can you venture a guess as to the overall percentage of growth?
- Can you provide more detail regarding the company's products and services? Are there plans for any new products or services? What do you consider to be the organization's greatest assets?
- How would you rate the company against its competitors? What competitive advantages does the company have? Is the company vulnerable in any areas relative to its competition? Why is the company unique in the market?
- Can you describe the company's overall management style?
- What is the company's overall communication style to its employees? Can you let me know what specific means they use to achieve this?
- What is your organization's policy regarding transfers to other cities?
- What is the employee turnover ratio?

- Can you describe the benefits the company provides (health-care insurance, dental, profit sharing, 401(k) match, and so forth)?
- Does the company typically pay bonuses? If so, what has been the historical trend?

Role

- Why is the position open? If it is a newly created position, why was it created? If it is replenishment for a vacancy, why did the previous employee leave or why did you let the previous employee go?
- Can you provide more detail on the primary and secondary responsibilities and any other pertinent information you think would be helpful so that I have an accurate view of the job?
- What are the performance expectations of this position over the first twelve months?
- How many people work in the unit and specifically what types of function do they perform?
- How does upper management view the role and importance of this unit?
- What are the characteristics of the most successful individuals within the company and this particular team?
- What types of skills do you not already have on the team that you would like to fill with the new hire?
- How much autonomy is there for me to make key decisions within this role?
- Have you interviewed any other candidates for the role? If you haven't yet hired someone, what was lacking in those individuals? If someone rejected your employment offer, why did they do that?
- What are the various ways employees communicate with one another to carry out their work?

- How and by whom will my performance be reviewed? Are there specific criteria upon which I would be evaluated? And how frequently is formal and informal review given to new employees?
- Can you highlight the possibilities for growth beyond this position?
- How much support or assistance is made available to individuals in developing career goals?
- Does the organization support external training for this position? If so, how much expenditure is the company willing to support?
- How much travel is expected? Can you describe the amount, patterns, and typical locations?
- How is the compensation structured for this position? If there is a bonus opportunity, has that bonus been paid in previous years? If so, what portion has the bonus been paid (of the 100 percent available)? (Stay away from asking specifically how much the job pays.)
- What particular computer equipment and software do you use?

Boss

- What is your management style?
- Can you describe the characteristics and qualities of your most successful subordinates?
- What drew you to the organization?
- What has kept you here?
- Have you had to fire anyone from the unit? If so, can you describe that situation for me?

Interviewer

- Who does the position report to and can you describe that individual for me?

- If you were to offer me a job and I was to accept, what would be the first act I could do to make your life easier?
- Can you highlight for me something you discovered after you started that you were unaware of during your recruitment process (good or bad)?
- What are the top five things you would improve about the organization?
- What do you love most/least about working here?
- Do you have any reservations about hiring me?
- What are the next steps?

Closing Time

I close when I walk in the door. And I never stop
closing until I pull the door shut on my way out.

There are a million funny and quirky quotes about "closing." There
is the well-known ABC model for salespeople—Always Be Closing.
The first one that actually came to my mind as I began writing
this chapter was the monologue by Alec Baldwin's character in the
movie *Glengarry Glen Ross*. He rants for several minutes to a room
full of real estate agents, saying, "Coffee's for closers only." Since I
wanted the subheadings to be my thoughts, I simply started typing,
and that's what came out. My suggestion would be to follow that
approach throughout your entire interview and recruitment process.
Just make sure to be sincere about it the whole way through. You
don't want people to figuratively slap the checkered sports coat on
you so often adorned by the used car salesman.

If you've presented yourself well throughout the interview, you
will be in a strong position to do two critical closing acts. First,
you want to make sure the interviewer does not leave the room
with any doubt you are the right person for the job. Second, you
want to know the outcome before you leave.

*Reservations come in one of three forms. Your goal is to
eliminate two of them and soften the third.*

I'm a huge fan of open-ended questions. They get the interviewer
talking and help you explore areas in which you might not have
ventured. The end of the interview, however, is not the time to be
asking open-ended questions. It is the time to be sure you gather
any insight regarding how the interviewer feels about you and
eliminate any misunderstandings (remember those?).

I have toyed with this for years, constantly looking for the
most economical, bulletproof question to ask toward the end of
the interview. I have determined that *"Do you have any reservations
about hiring me?"* is the closest thing to perfection. I recognize that
some people will consider this a negative question. Others might
prefer a softer approach with something such as "Is there anything
else you'd like to know about me?" or "Is there anything I can
clarify?" or "How do you feel I match up for the job?" While all
of these are nice questions, they leave entirely too much room for
the interviewer to skirt the issue you ultimately need answered,
which is "Why won't you hire me?"

When inquiring about the specific reservations, you narrow the
scope of the information you want. You need to be very specific
that you want to know her *reservations*. While it is nice to know
where you scored well, generally speaking companies don't hire
you because of what they *think* you can't do rather than what you
can do. This "reservation" question serves as a safety net and allows
you to clarify any communication gaps the interviewer might have.
Her reservations typically come in one of three forms:

- Misunderstanding something you said
- Complete blind spot from an area she didn't
  investigate
- Valid reservation because of something you did or
  said, skill gap, and so on

If she misunderstood you, you are now in a position to clarify your original message. In the event she drew an incorrect conclusion because she didn't have the time to investigate key portions of your work experience, you can now highlight the experience you have in that area. The second issue is quite common. Interviewers simply assume you don't have the experience if *they* didn't ask you about it. Of course, there is always a chance that the interviewer has a valid reservation. At least at this point, you know it and can determine how to address it. I often recommend ending on a high note by confirming how you would eliminate that actual reservation. The most important part of this closing technique is ensuring that the interviewer leaves with no doubt you are the right person for the job.

No one likes to make a decision independently anymore.
Help reassure the interviewer it is okay to hire you.

It seems to me that people have trouble making decisions for themselves. It doesn't matter whether it's what shirt to buy or what car to lease. Hiring decisions are one of the touchiest decisions that an employer faces, especially because no one wants to inherit the blame for a faulty hire. You need to reassure every single interviewer in the process that hiring you is the right decision. They literally need encouragement from you that it is okay. How do you do that?

The first thing you need to do is gain control of the interview. This is usually not too difficult at the end, because either you are in your question-asking period or the interviewer will transfer it to you with, "Is there anything else?" or "Do you have any more questions for me?" Regardless of the entry point, you can do three things to provide them the encouragement they need: Confirm, Assure, and Close.

Confirm: You want to restate your understanding of what the employer needs. This serves two purposes. First, it leaves the employer with the impression that you truly understand the position and therefore can make an educated decision to join the company. It will also uncover any gaps you have in your understanding of the position. Once you have stated your understanding or have received clarity, you can proceed to assuring them of your strengths and fit. For example: "I want to confirm that you are looking for someone with strong [insert skills and experience here] to work on [insert responsibilities here]. Is that correct? [Let the interviewer confirm your assumption or clarify.] If so, I'd like to recap my strengths."

Assure: You can now literally repeat your strengths as they relate to the requirements and align to the job responsibilities. For example: "As we discussed during the interview, I have extensive experience in [insert a brief recap of those strengths you touched upon during the session]. I believe that helps you see I am an ideal candidate for the position."

Close: Confirm for the interviewer that based on what they need and offer and your match of experience with the requirements of the position, you are very interested in the job and company. It also helps to show that you are confident you will perform well. Follow this up with a question regarding next steps. For example: "Because we are such as great fit, I want you to know that I am extremely interested the job. Is there anything else I can provide to help with your decision? What would be the next step in the process?"

Doesn't anyone take the time to send a card anymore?

I'm guessing that if I bought every candidate a little box of thank-you cards and requested they use them only for prospective employers they've interviewed with, they would never run out.

Somewhere along the way, e-mail has virtually eliminated the use of handwritten cards to express "Thanks for taking the time to interview me." I might be old-fashioned, but I think that there are two things that carry weight when expressing gratitude: speed and thoughtfulness.

First, you want to make sure to send a thank-you note as quickly as possible following your interview. Speed indicates interest. Lack of speed usually indicates lack of interest. It is typically most effective to express thanks as well as your feelings about the position while still fresh in your mind. This makes it easier for you to pinpoint specific remarks you discussed. Since snail mail is slower to reach the interviewer, I suggest sending an e-mail the same day of your interview (and make sure you can spell-check it). This will ensure the interviewer can factor in your favorable thank-you message when providing feedback to the appropriate person. I also suggest sending a handwritten note as well because it requires more energy, making it inherently much more thoughtful.

Regarding the content of your thank you, make sure to begin with words of thanks followed by a brief recap of a few of the most critical points. You do not and should not relive the entire interview in written form. The main points for your recap should focus on your match for the job. This will also make visible for the interviewer your match (remember reassurance). Complete the note with remarks confirming your interest in the position. If you intend to also send a handwritten note (which I strongly recommend), you might want to mention in the e-mail that you have also sent something in the mail but wanted to send a short e-mail for expediency's sake. Lastly, I would recommend that the length of the e-mail (or handwritten note) be short enough so they will read it but long enough to include relevant substance that will keep you fresh in their mind. Below is a sample to help illustrate the point:

Thank You Note: Hi John, thank you so much for taking the time to meet with me today. I appreciated the chance to learn more about *you* and the company.

Based on the key points we discussed today, I feel I would be a fantastic match for the job because [insert details here, but be sure this requires no more than two or three lines.]

Lastly, I want to reconfirm my interest in the position. After speaking with you, I was more excited about the opportunity because you verified the company supports my interests related to [insert specifics here].

Decision Time

You've been logical up until this point. Why become so emotional now?

In 2006, a protégé who I had worked with for several years while at my first company became a milewalk candidate. He had been with his current employer (my former employer) for approximately ten years or so. He had approached me because he felt it might be time for a change. I was happy to help.

We started discussing his current situation, opportunities for improvement, needs, and so on. I knew him well and had worked with him for several years, so we were able to build quite an accurate list of his requirements. There were several of them—which is important, because the more criteria you can define, the more certain you can be whether something fits for you. Matching nineteen of your twenty criteria often proves a better match than three for three.

One of my clients had a fabulous opportunity that matched his *entire* list of needs and wants—a smaller, more entrepreneurial company, chance to make a great impact, professional growth into a more senior position, chance to build a team, global experience, more pay, less travel, and so forth. Since it matched his interests and he was well-qualified from a skills perspective, it was an easy decision to engage him in their recruiting process.

He managed to complete the process, and they extended him an offer, which he formally accepted. He resigned from his current employer. Everything looked normal for the transition to the new company. Then he started to get cold feet. His employer prepared a counteroffer, which from an economical and professional standpoint did not approach my client's opportunity. You can imagine where this is going. A few weeks later, my client sent him a formal letter rescinding the offer because we couldn't reach him for a live discussion.

What's the moral of the story? From an outsider's point of view, the logical choice was to accept the new position. Logic, however, plays almost no part in changing jobs. No matter what form of logical reasoning you use, changing jobs is as emotional as getting married or buying your first house. People simply cannot reason themselves into a new job. They need to "feel" themselves into a new job. As I mentioned earlier, people would rather live with unhappiness than uncertainty. Apparently, for some reason, the right feel helps trump uncertainty.

Before we discuss how to channel the emotional aspect to work in your favor, let's discuss what is actually at issue here. First, there is nothing wrong with having emotions. Emotions are what often make us act, drive us, and lift us to new heights. The problem arises only when your emotions become uncontrollable, misguided, or unfounded and create fear or other manufactured falsities. Instead of letting your emotions run amuck, focus on your intuition. In my opinion, along with your self-awareness, intuition is your greatest asset to succeed throughout your career. This also reminds me of one of the many great quotes by Albert Einstein: "The intuitive mind is a sacred gift and the rational mind is a faithful servant. We have created a society that honors the servant and has forgotten the gift."

Let's toss "luck" in there while we're at it. I have read a number of articles and books related to luck. I always have wondered what makes lucky people lucky. Most of the material highlights common characteristics of lucky people. Of course, let's remove the underlying theme that if you think you're lucky, you are, and much of this has to do with your outlook on life. Positive-oriented people simply look on the bright side (e.g., I was in a car crash and walked out without scratch—whew, that was lucky). Beyond that, these people often share three common traits. First, they never give up. Second, they mix it up to maximize chance opportunities. Third, and in my opinion most importantly, they listen to their intuition and act quickly (not rashly). The simple fact is that your intuition has been formed through your life experience. It also serves as your "brain mechanism" to synthesize your decisions. Synthesizing allows you to look at the issue or decision as a whole. Analyzing, by contrast, causes you to look at the parts and break up the problem (not in a good way), and often causes a much more delayed response. There are certainly times when prudent analysis is called for. Changing jobs, however, requires careful synthesis, an intuition check, and a decisive response.

Before and during your interviewing process, you can improve your self-awareness and shape your intuition by reviewing and executing the principles highlighted in the first chapter. If you prepared those guidelines for yourself in advance, you are now better positioned to make a sound choice when the employer extends the job offer. If you did not, you risk rationalizing the most critical pieces of information required to make a good decision. If you have not done so yet, I would encourage you to perform the following activities when you receive your employment offer:

- Evaluate your current situation according to the guidelines highlighted earlier.
- Reflect on your key decision points throughout your career (job transitions, etc.).
- Reexamine and update your Value Package Criteria, which confirms your requirements.

- Match the job's offerings to your Value Package Criteria.
- Review your timing considerations.
- Weigh the offered compensation against your current actual (not your perceived) market value.
- Talk with your spouse (if applicable).

Notice I did not include speak with mentors, confidants, or other trusted advisors. I'm sure most of you will ignore that advice, but I classify seeking counsel of this nature as analyzing as opposed to synthesizing your decision. Here's why. You have just spent several days, weeks, or months interviewing with an organization. You have supplemented that dialog with research you've performed. While I'm not exactly sure how much of your time this consumed, I'm fairly certain it will be substantially more than the few minutes you'll spend relaying the situation to a friend or coworker. Your storytelling to them will likely be somewhat tainted (unintentionally) by your biases toward the confirmation you seek. Throwing in the fact that they likely do not know the employer or your complete list of needs leaves you with additional insight you can do without. Trust yourself more than you trust anyone else. It'll serve you better. If nothing else, it's easier to live with your own "mistakes" than someone else's. Chances are, if you did your homework, you'll make the right choice either way.

They just asked me how much money I want. What do I do?

You know that expression often used in sales negotiations, "He who speaks first, loses"? Well, that doesn't always apply in negotiating your employment offer. There are so many factors to consider, the first of which is when the employer inquires about compensation.

The most important success factor in achieving what you want is making sure to request it when your "stock" is highest. This is unlikely to be during the first interview. You simply haven't had enough opportunity to dazzle them. If it is, you won't be in the process very long nor need to be concerned about this. So, if during the first interview, the employer asks your desired level of compensation, I would recommend responding with something such as, "Here is my current level of compensation. I am certain if we are the right match for each other we will be able to come to an agreement that's amenable for both of us." You've now provided the company with valuable data (if they didn't have it already). Keep in mind, the more they like you, the more they're willing to pay. The more you like them, the less you're willing to accept. (In the same vein, I don't recommend employers explaining up front what the position pays. In the same manner the candidate has not had a chance to impress the company, the company has not had a chance to impress the candidate. The candidate might, in fact, be willing to negotiate away dollars for the pure joy of working there. She doesn't know that yet because she has very little information.)

If the employer indicates they would like to extend an offer to you, position yourself to review the offer in its entirety. Review your current situation, requirements, timing constraints, and compensation. Take a close look not only at the potential compensation level but also at the company outlook, culture, role, professional development, coworkers, autonomy, work and life balance, location, travel, and benefits.

Perhaps the most important thing to remember at this stage is that as soon as the employer announces it would like to extend you an offer, you have instantaneously become teammates—not adversaries—in the negotiation. You either both win (if you accept) or both lose (if you do not). What do teammates do? By connotation, they work together to accomplish a common goal. That means communicating with each other to express your needs, areas that are important to you, where you can be flexible, and your rationale for wanting certain components in your overall compensation package. To the extent you can convey to them that you "want to make this work," you will substantially increase the likelihood of realizing what you want.

How much "think time" should I request?

This is a critical decision, so make sure to request the appropriate amount of time to consider it. There is no one set industry standard for the duration. The most important factor is to provide the company with a definitive date you will respond—and stick to it.

If you need a few days, you can simply indicate so and respond at the appropriate time (or before) with a verbal, e-mailed, or written confirmation. I recommend the verbal response, especially considering the magnitude, but also realize all situations are different.

If you need a few weeks, I recommend agreeing to a touchpoint with the employer sometime in between so as not to have an extended period of silence. This checkpoint serves as good opportunity for both parties to ask questions or provide clarifications.

The Breakup

There's no such thing as a good breakup.

Let's assume you accepted the new company's offer to join. It's time to resign. The most important part about resigning is that you are definitive and clear regarding your commitment (not just your intention) to leave.

I suggest preparing a resignation letter that includes a few critical pieces of information: a thank you, confirmation of your resignation, and your last date of employment. This is not only the classy thing to do, it will also look favorable in the file should you ever consider returning.

Thank You: Thank your employer for all the opportunity it has provided you. Regardless of whether you are happy or sad to leave, realize you have gained invaluable experiences. Appreciate them.

Confirm Resignation: Include the position from which you are resigning with definitive language stating that you have accepted another position. Do not include any language that implies you are open to considering your current employer's input regarding this matter. This will be construed as either wavering or a ploy on your part to see whether they will upgrade your pay or provide other enticements to stay.

Last Date: Specify your last date of employment. This date can be determined based on a few factors. In some instances, you might have an employment agreement that legally cites the minimum period you are required to stay from the date you provide resignation notice. Others might want to factor the appropriate amount of time for knowledge transfer to other employees or wrap up remaining projects. A typical resignation period is between two and four weeks, but the majority are shorter. Whatever the length of the period, realize the longer the gap between your acceptance and start dates for your new job, the less likely you are to show up—whether this was your choice or your new employer's. Given time, things simply come up.

After you've prepared your letter and are ready to resign, I would be sure to gather your personal belongings or computer files in the event your employer immediately walks you to the door after receiving your notice. This is as rare in some industries as it is common in others. You will be the best judge of what you're likely to encounter, but I recommend being prepared for anything.

When resigning, I would discuss it verbally before handing the appropriate person your letter. When you convey this message verbally, be sure to use definitive words and language such as "I have already accepted another offer." Stay away from expressions such as, "I'm considering another offer," because that leaves room for your employer to misinterpret your intentions.

Whether you are providing your verbal or written resignation, make sure to avoid mud-slinging or unconstructive remarks that could be construed as frustration. No good can come of this. If you care to provide constructive feedback for your current employer, you will likely have the opportunity to present it during an exit interview. During that time, keep the remarks upbeat and professional.

Should I prepare for the kitchen sink?

No one likes to be fired, especially not employers. For the most part, employers, especially those with which you have developed a lengthy, successful relationship, will be disappointed when you resign. They will likely want to understand your rationale. Sometimes they want to understand it to determine whether there is something they can do to keep you. Other times, they are simply looking for feedback and improvements they can channel into the remaining employee base. If you feel it necessary to engage in this dialog, you are best suited to discuss points that the new employer offers that your current one simply cannot. That usually helps avoid the back-and-forth of "what if we do this or that?"

Wait! Don't Leave!

Accepting a counteroffer grants you a shelf-life of six to twelve months.

It's not over yet. Unfortunately, all too often, employers feel compelled to present departing employees with a counteroffer. As soon as you accept the counteroffer—a *true* counteroffer—you may as well start interviewing again.

There are many forms of counteroffers. I only consider a counteroffer true if your current employer extends it *after* you have already accepted a position with another company and have *resigned* from your current organization with genuine *intent* to leave. There are many variations from what I just described. For example, you could have made your current employer aware of an offer you received but didn't accept. I classify this situation (and others like it) as silly maneuvers to gain leverage in reinforcing your value to the company. Candidly, the detrimental impact of these latter situations does not carry the same level of gravity to both parties that a true counteroffer does. The reason is that a threat never hurts as much as reality.

There are many emotional and economical factors at play whenever a company decides to present an employee with a counteroffer. I'd like to review them in detail to help you manage this delicate and often gut-wrenching situation.

First, it's emotional—again.

Typically, whenever an employee resigns, the company feels hurts. Remember, these are human beings with feelings. Your boss and management team will initially feel as though this is a reflection on them. Even if nothing could be further from the truth, people are generally self-centered when it comes to situations like this. They are inclined to feel as though you are quitting them as opposed to the company. Based on probability and the statistics I've previously provided, you likely are quitting them, but there can certainly be a host of other reasons.

Regardless of what happens next, remember you have damaged the relationship—at least temporarily. The company might pull it together quickly and attempt to address your issues. You need to recognize that good, well-managed organizations never, under any circumstances, present counteroffers. They don't need to because they have universal policies and procedures that are equitable for all employees. They provide strong compensation programs. Most importantly, they recognize no one is irreplaceable—not even you— so they nurture their existing employee base for successions when employees leave. They also execute strong recruiting programs so they can hire additional resources when appropriate. To present a counteroffer to an employee would likely require them to break protocol, something great organizations simply don't do.

Your emotions are a different story. While theirs start in the dumpster and rise if they succeed in retaining you, yours are initially elevated from the high that they desire you. Of course, you have immediately forgotten that two days ago, you were feeling unappreciated, undervalued, underpaid, or whatever else drove you to this situation in the first place. Don't worry, the laws of the universe have an incredibly tenacious way of balancing themselves, so you're in for a letdown soon enough. How do I know? Because after the heightened emotions are addressed in the initial renegotiation, you are left with a situation where you need to perform under what I call the "post-counteroffer-promotion" syndrome. You know that situation. It's the one where someone is now paid more (or has received alternate concessions), has the same level of skills they did yesterday, and is expected to do more in a shorter period of time, under the watchful eye of a jilted boss, while the management team looks for your replacement so they're not out the entire annual raise they provided you. You will be brought back to earth quickly enough.

As your descent speeds up, they too are falling from their high of saving you. Now they simply view you as disloyal. The good news for them is they now have more time to replace you. As time goes on, you recognize that you wanted to leave for more reasons than simply money, and you become unhappy again. If you don't leave soon of your own accord, they will likely replace you. I combed the books and Internet for various statistics regarding counteroffers. I found many various viewpoints but most indicated that over 80 percent of individuals who accept a counteroffer from their current employer are no longer with that company after six months. The National Employment Association gives that number as 89 percent. Do you want those odds?

After the emotions calm down, it's truly about the economics.

Let's say for the sake of argument that you let your emotions overwhelm you, and you are strongly considering the counteroffer. Have you thought about the implications for the company if they've provided you an unexpected pay raise?

You just made the employer dip into its coffer for more money. Last time I checked, businesses survive by making a profit. I'm not saying your pay raise is going to bring down the house, but I'm fairly confident your employer will find some way to recuperate funds it didn't expect to spend. There are many ways to look at it, but your $5,000 pay raise could amount to a mere $833 if they replace you within two months. That's before the government removes your taxes. Perhaps they do keep you around. Your next cost of living raise might be significantly reduced (or eliminated altogether). Both of these previous scenarios assume your employer had the money to give you in the first place. Where did they get it and why didn't they give it to you before you threatened to leave?

Do you have any pride or integrity?

So you've been overcome with emotion, and you're not very good at math. Both of these can be excused. What about your integrity? What about your pride? Let's take a cold, hard look at what is transpiring. You have decided to leave your current employer, probably for good reasons. You have accepted a new position, agreed to it, and signed a formal offer. You have committed! You are about to squander your honor and break your word (and your signature).

Regarding your current employer, you are now officially an extortionist. You can rationalize it any way you want. It also doesn't matter how nice and sweet you are. You have technically extorted more money or concessions. It's that simple. You need to be more worried about why you work for an organization that requires these tactics from you in order to pay you appropriately. If your current company relents and succumbs to your extortion, they are just as bad. Even worse than the extortion, you have given your word to a new innocent party. You are about to break that. That's entirely your doing.

If all that isn't bad enough . . .

If you've accepted a counteroffer, you might think the damage is contained to your current company and the jilted prospective employer. You might think the world is big enough for this to go away. I've learned the world can be quite small. If you are a specialist in an industry, it will be smaller. If you are a senior-level executive in a particular sector, it will be smaller still. People talk. They change companies. Word gets out. Don't even get me started on recruiters, corporate and agency alike, who seem all too happy to share with their fellow recruiters and companies references regarding individuals who accept counteroffers. Even if people avoid holding this against you, there is also karma. Karma seems to have the best memory of all.

Out of the other side of mouth . . .

I'm happy to be fair. There might be rare instances when accepting the counteroffer is the smart thing to do. Perhaps you were overly emotional when you started interviewing with the new employer or there was a drastic change of events that occurred during the process. Maybe you've had more to time think and things weren't as bad as you thought.

I have seen a select few instances where individuals have accepted counteroffers and gone on to several more productive and enjoyable years with their employer. Keep in mind, however, that is more the exception than the rule. I suggest you think deeply about the reasons you initiated the process. A counteroffer is typically unlikely to address those reasons in the long run.

If You Interview Today

I'd like to wrap this book up with a reference guide in the event you are interviewing at the moment (or plan to in the near future). Let's take a look at how to prepare, execute, and follow up.

Preparation makes up for many talent shortcomings.

Before the interview, prepare for all facets you might encounter. Keep in mind, you are putting together a plan that will allow you to effectively execute the interview, but it will also provide you with the freedom to make alterations when necessary.

Evaluate Yourself

Perform your current assessment to ensure you can effectively determine whether the opportunity is right for you:

- Current Situation. Identify all forms of what you currently have
- Requirements. Develop a list of your needs and wants
- Timing Considerations. Determine whether now is an appropriate time to leave
- Counteroffer Potential. Prepare in advance whether you would entertain this
- Compensation and Benefits. Review a complete list of your current actual value

Research the Company

Research the organization to ensure you are fully prepared to respond effectively to its interviewing questions as well as use the information to prepare your questions.

- Review corporate website
- Review additional websites such as LinkedIn, Glassdoor, Vault, WetFeet, and Hoovers
- Discover key information such as the following:
  - o Why would I want to work there?
  - o Does the company have a product or service that is valuable?
  - o Is the company a leader in its industry?
  - o What is the corporate culture and is it unique?
  - o What are the job and career development opportunities?
  - o Who works there?
  - o What are the benefits?

Review the Interviewer

Perform research on the interviewer(s) (if known) to determine common acquaintances, interests, and so forth. Review websites such as LinkedIn as well as perform simple Google searches.

Remember the Key Success Factors

Be mindful of the reasons you will be successful during the interview. Focus on your ability to *accurately articulate* your qualifications and potential contribution. Begin preparing your stories so they help the *interviewer accurately interpret* your responses as well as *remember* them.

Prepare for Likely Interview Questions

Review the areas you anticipate will be most important to the interviewer as well as the common effective interviewing questions.

- Review the two types of questions ("What would you do?" and "What did you do?")
- Review your background to refresh your memory on the details of your career highlights
- Review the six common qualities for effective, memorable storytelling:
    - o Keep it short and simple
    - o Capture and keep their attention
    - o Talk in their lingo
    - o Make them believe you
    - o Get them to care
    - o Get them to act
- Use the fourteen effective interviewing questions to prepare appropriate responses, including the six key qualities for memorable responses

Prepare Your Questions

Review your current situation, interests, requirements, and other relevant information to prepare effective questions to ask the interviewer. Categorize your questions to demonstrate your organization skills and portray your team-player orientation.

- Group questions accordingly—Company, Role, Boss (or Interviewer)
- Use sample questions included in this book as a starting point
- Identify your additional questions as appropriate
- Structure questions to maximize benefit to you— Passion, Smarts, Intelligence

Execution is easy when you're honest and interested.

During the interview, execute as you have prepared. Even if the interviewer surprises you with unanticipated questions, your level of preparation will position you to effectively handle them.

"Friend" the Interviewer

During the opening moments, use opportunities to shrink the world, if appropriate. Keep your eyes and ears open for clues as to the interviewer's interests.

Tell Effective Stories

Use the principles outlined for storytelling, including the six qualities for memorable stories, to respond to the interview questions.

Ask Profitable Questions

Use the three elements of effective questioning when asking the interviewer—Passion, Smarts, and Intelligence.

Close Well

Assess the interviewer's reservations to allay them. Confirm for the interviewer that you are the right candidate for the job. Ensure you leave the interview with an understanding of next steps.

- Ask the ultimate closing question: "Do you have any reservations about hiring me?"
- Evaluate the interviewer's reservations.
- Address any misinterpretations or communication gaps.
- Reassure the interviewer using the Confirm, Assure, and Close technique.

Always be appreciative and thankful.

Follow Up with Thank You

Follow up that same day with effective thank-you techniques. Send e-mail and confirm you're mailing a personalized handwritten note. Thank-you note should start with thanks for your time, follow with points aligning you to the position, and close with confirmation of your interest.

INDEX OF THOUGHTS

"Friending" the interviewer—the best techniques to develop a connection with the interviewer.

Storytelling and the six qualities that make your responses memorable—keep it short and simple, capture and keep their attention, talk in their lingo, make them believe you, get them to care, and get them to act.

My silver bullet interview—fourteen key interviewing questions, the rationale behind them, and effective responses.

Question organizing—the most effective way to categorize your questions into the three main groups: Company, Role, and Boss (or Interviewer).

Question asking—the most effective way to structure your specific questions to show passion, smarts, and intelligence.

Question samples—examples for the main categories of Company, Role, and Boss (or Interviewer).

Closing an interview—detecting the interviewer's reservations about hiring you.

Closing an interview with the Confirm, Assure, Close technique—reassuring the interviewer that it is okay to hire you.

Interview follow up—thank-you response techniques.

Evaluating the employment offer—reviewing your previously prepared information and the job offer to make an educated decision regarding whether to accept it.

Resigning from your current employer—techniques to properly provide verbal and written notice to leave your job.

Resisting the counteroffer from your current employer—issues related to accepting your current employer's appeal to keep you.

Chapter 11
93

Interview process reference guide—overall checklist of key concepts and activities to ensure success in your interviewing process.

Chapter 12
98

RECOMMENDED READING

Bolles, Richard. *What Color Is Your Parachute?* Ten Speed Press, 1970

Ferriss, Timothy. *The 4-Hour Workweek.* Crown Publishing Group, 2007

Gilbert, Daniel. *Stumbling on Happiness.* Random House, 2005

Godin, Seth. *The Dip.* Penguin Group, 2007

Goleman, Daniel. *Emotional Intelligence: Why It Can Matter More Than IQ.* Bantam, 1995

Heath, Chip and Heath, Dan. *Made to Stick.* Random House, 2007

Lucht, John. *Rites of Passage at $100,000 to $1 Million+.* Viceroy Press, 2001

RECOMMENDED WEBSITES

Glassdoor: www.glassdoor.com

Hoovers: www.hoovers.com

LinkedIn: www.linkedin.com

milewalk Inc.: www.milewalk.com

Securities & Exchange Commission, Edgar: www.sec.gov/edgar/searchedgar/webusers.htm

Vault Career Intelligence: www.vault.com

WetFeet: www.wetfeet.com

AFTERWORD

For me, finished was better than perfect.

I could have made this book three times as long and continued developing it for years with the hope of "perfecting" it. It was far more important to me to complete it and get it in your hands. I am absolutely positive there are many other great points and techniques that could have been included. You are certainly welcome to contact me if you would like to share your thoughts.

I also welcome all inquires related to milewalk's services in helping your organization. Feel free to contact me regarding meetings, speaking engagements, insight for your recruiters and interviewers, recruitment services, or other offerings.

For all correspondences, please e-mail to info@milewalk. com. Looking forward to hearing from you!

ABOUT THE AUTHOR

Andrew LaCivita is a world-leading career and hiring expert. He is the award-winning author of three books, including *The Hiring Prophecies: Psychology behind Recruiting Successful Employees* and *Out of Reach but in Sight: Using Goals to Achieve Your Impossible.* He has dedicated his life to helping people and companies realize their potential. Visit him at andrewlacivita.com and milewalkacademy.com.